The Joy
of Spiritual Living

The Joy
of Spiritual Living

Simple Steps to Your Best Self

Frank Rose and Bob Maginel

SWEDENBORG FOUNDATION

West Chester, Pennsylvania

Tasks and guidelines described in this book were developed by the authors for the Spiritual Growth Program at Sunrise Chapel in Tucson, Arizona. Inquiries about this program may be directed to:
Arizona Spiritual Growth Foundation, Inc.
8421 E. Wrightstown Road
Tucson, AZ 85715

Library of Congress Cataloging-in-Publication Data

Rose, Frank, 1927–
    The joy of spiritual living : simple steps to your best self /
        Frank Rose and Bob Maginel.
        pages cm
    Includes bibliographical references.
    ISBN 978-0-87785-352-7 (pbk.)
1. Spiritual life. 2. New Jerusalem Church. I. Maginel, Robert. II. Title.
    BL624.R655 2014
    248.4'894--dc23

                                2014020015

Scripture quotations from John 16:33 are taken from the New King James Version®. Copyright © 1982 by Thomas Nelson. Used by permission. All rights reserved.

All other scripture quotations contained herein are from the New Revised Standard Version Bible, copyright © 1989 by the Division of Christian Education of the National Council of the Churches of Christ in the U.S.A., and are used by permission. All rights reserved.

Edited by Lisa Lapp
Design and typesetting by Karen Connor
Cover art by Mia Bosna

Printed in the United States of America

Swedenborg Foundation
320 North Church Street • West Chester, PA 19380
www.swedenborg.com

We dedicate this book to all those "teachers" in our
lives who have aided us on our spiritual journeys.
We are especially grateful to those who have shared
their emotions, thoughts, and wisdom with us over the
years in our Spiritual Growth Group meetings.

When people of good intention share their innermost
thoughts and feelings, those who listen with open
minds and loving hearts are the true beneficiaries.
We know we are the better for sharing our journeys
with such exceptional people. Thank you all for what
you have taught us.

CONTENTS

INTRODUCTION TO JOYFUL LIVING

We all want a joyful life. We want to live in harmony with others, experience our own self-worth, and enjoy safety and order in our world. We all want peace of mind. But life bombards us with negativity. News and social media bring us instant word of strife and disaster from around the world. In our personal lives, all types of conflicts, aggravations, and crises trigger negative reactions within us. It seems the world is determined to disrupt our connection with joy.

How can we achieve joyful living amid this daily assault on our inner peace?

We might isolate ourselves from the world, and seek joy in solitude. After all, solitary meditation and prayer are important components of a joyful life.

But joyful living happens *in* life, not apart from it. In our decades of work with spiritual growth groups, we have found that inner growth is an active process that happens in real-life moments, and that shutting out the external world is not the key to joy.

This work has taught us that our own negativity is actually an "inside job." The problem is that our negative reactions arise from within us and take hold, cutting us off from joy.

Our challenge, then, is to stay engaged with life while we work to rise above our own negative reactions, grow step by step into our best self, and achieve the joy of spiritual living.

A STRUCTURED SPIRITUAL GROWTH PROGRAM

Each task presented in this book is a step in our structured program of spiritual growth. These simple tasks, when practiced consciously in everyday life, can help unlock our inner growth at the very moment when negativity arises—when our ego charges in and wants control. We hope you will use the tasks in this book as tools to help you choose joy, and reject negativity, in your own real-life moments of choice.

We have found that, with this kind of practice, we can learn to respond to life from a higher place in ourselves, until that higher place feels more and more like where we live. This is what we mean by spiritual growth.

All tasks and tools in this book are drawn from the materials we have developed in our work leading spiritual growth groups and seminars sponsored by the Arizona Spiritual Growth Foundation. Our program, begun in 1988 by a small group of fellow travelers, is based at Sunrise Chapel in Tucson.

Our earlier book, *The Joy of Spiritual Growth* (1999), presents other tasks from the same program. That book may be used in tandem with this one, or either book may be used alone.

BASIC CONCEPTS

Our program's tasks and exercises are based on the teachings of Swedish scientist-turned-seer Emanuel Swedenborg (1688–1772). In Swedenborg's writings about spiritual growth, he likens our mind to a house with many floors. We may reside in the "basement," where the beasts of anger, fear, jealousy, depression, resentment, and many other negative emotions reside. Or we may choose to climb the stairs to our upper floors, where exist the love, peace, and happiness that we all seek.

Using Swedenborg's model, this program offers tasks that can help lead you upward, out of the basement, to the joy of living in the glow of your Higher Power's love. Put more simply, this program fosters a more loving view of yourself and others in your life.

Though our philosophy is decidedly Christian, you need not subscribe to a particular faith to use our program's tasks for your own inner growth. Some skill at loving self-observation and self-awareness, however, is key. Honest awareness of one's own behavior and state of being is critical to spiritual growth.

Please note that this program is not designed as a way to deal with deep psychological or emotional problems, uncontrolled addictions, or abusive relationships. If you are struggling with a serious issue, you should seek help to resolve the issue before you join us on the spiritual journey in this book.

HOW TO USE THIS BOOK

This book is set up as a manual for personal growth, with tasks and exercises accompanied by discussion of the specific challenges of each task, and supplemental passages for further insight.

An important feature of this program is the opportunity to share your own experience with others who are grappling with similar challenges in their spiritual growth. You can gain much wisdom by working these tasks with a group of kindred souls. That is why, in these pages, we have included transcribed discussions from sessions of a recent spiritual growth seminar, whose participants have agreed to share their experience and insights with you. Please regard these group participants as fellow travelers on your spiritual journey.

Each of us in these transcribed group sessions has made a sincere effort to tell you what happened in our lives and how we reacted to each task. You'll notice that sometimes we failed to react the ways we thought we should have—but that failure is also a learning experience and an important step in the journey of spiritual growth.

If you are working with your own group, please take advantage of the materials provided in the appendix. If no group is available to you, consider yourself a member of the group in this book. As you work on your own inner growth, a sense of fellowship along the way can help you realize that we all deal with similar issues.

The Joy
of Spiritual Living

Task 1

EXPLORE THE LEVELS OF YOUR HOUSE

 For this first week, focus on the human mind as a "house of spiritual awareness." When you experience an emotion, take a moment to notice on which level of your "house" the emotion resides.

- If you discover that your emotion resides in the lower levels of your "house," see if your awareness, by itself, shines enough light on that "beast in your basement" to lessen its impact on your spiritual well-being.

- When you experience a negative emotion, reflect on parts of your life that you experience in a higher, more joyful place. See if your thoughts of more joyful experience bring peace to replace the negative focus of your thoughts.

- Journal about your experience with this task.

- For groups: Come to your next group meeting prepared to share the impact of any new awareness you have experienced.

Learning Objectives
- *Understand the concept of the spiritual dimension of life.*
- *Become familiar with the "house of spiritual awareness" as a model of the mind.*
- *Understand that uncritical self-awareness and loving self-observation are essential to your spiritual growth.*

In our first task, we examine how we can raise ourselves to the higher levels of life experience. We begin with awareness. Once we become aware that we exist as spiritual beings on several levels, we can learn how to move from the mind's lower levels to its higher levels, where joy and peace reside.

Emanuel Swedenborg has offered a model of the mind that looks like a house with several floors or stories. The floors are connected by stairways that allow us to move from one level to the next. These stairways represent our access to higher levels of spiritual joy in our life. They represent the vertical dimension through which we commune with our Higher Power.

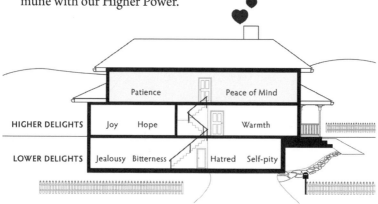

Get to know your mind as a "house of spiritual awareness."

At the lowest level of our house of spiritual awareness is our basement. The negative emotions reside here and can quickly take control of our lives. Here we find self-pity, jealously, bitterness, hatred, and all other negative emotions that rapidly drag us down into a negative state of mind.

In the higher levels of the house we find joy, hope, warmth, peace of mind, and patience. These are the emotions that our Higher Power wishes us to experience.

This book is about raising ourselves above the basement emotions to experience the joy of living on the level of peace and love.

How can we use this model to raise our own life experience to a higher level? First we have to know where we are coming from. We must notice when we are having an emotional reaction to a life experience, and this takes awareness.

Awareness is the cornerstone of spiritual growth.

Wouldn't it be wonderful if we could be vaccinated against the negatives that invade our lives? If we could become immune to negative emotions, life would be fairly simple. But, alas, there is no such immunity. We must learn how to deal within ourselves with life's offerings.

That is what we like about our spiritual growth program. Spiritual growth is all about how you deal with your own life's offerings, on your own terms.

Does this sound selfish? We believe it is not so selfish when, by learning to keep negative emotions from interfering with your own joy, you also unlock the joy you can bring to those around you. We believe this is what our Higher Power intended for us as our mission and purpose in life.

In this program, simply waking up and becoming aware of your spiritual self is the most important first step in improving your spiritual life. When you are spiritually asleep and don't recognize the negative emotions that control some of your actions, you become a victim of those negative emotions. Our Higher Power tells us to watch and wake up—to protect *ourselves* from the negatives that invade our lives.

Once we were approached by a man with a pertinent question. This gentleman was a brain surgeon—he understood the composition and function of the human brain—and he asked, "How can I explain to my young son that emotional reaction is so much quicker than rational thought?"

His question highlights that our reactions to emotional stimuli take hold well before our intellect can reason its way through the situation that triggered the reaction. Perhaps this is akin to the "fight or flight" reaction that we learn about in basic psychology—we are wired to react before we think. This happens far too often in my life, and the results are often disastrous.

Here are two examples of how negative emotions take control of our responses:

1. Imagine a couple who has had a successful and loving marriage entering into an argument about some trivial matter. They argue about something as trivial as how each remembered an event in their past.

   Sometimes simple disagreements on trivial matters create animosity and anger that control both parties and how they react. But does the emotion of that moment, that anger that exists for just a moment in time, reflect the loving relationship this couple has had for years? I don't think so. Yet for that brief moment, anger is the dominant emotion and love is pushed out of the way. Not a rational thought enters the equation of that moment in their relationship!

2. The same can be said about a parent and a child. In a moment of displeasure with the child's actions, the parent may raise a hand, or their voice, toward the child in anger. Does this moment of anger represent the sum total of the relationship between parent and child? I don't think so.

   The anger may pass quickly, and the parent and child may return to a relationship of nurture and mutual respect, but sometimes the damage is done. When negative emotion takes control, love and understanding are pushed to the background. The "beasts" are out of the basement!

So let's return to our model of the mind as a house. The lower levels of our house hold negative emotions that can rapidly destroy our respectful and loving relationships. We must move up, out of the basement and into our higher levels to regain joy, peace, and contentment. This is what spiritual growth is all about.

The simple tool that allows us to move out of the basement is *awareness.* This tool is as simple as a flashlight. When we shine a conscious light on the negative emotions that control our actions, just the awareness that those emotions exist will mitigate their strength. Just as critters of the night shy away from a beaming flashlight, the beasts in our basement lose power when we become aware of them and apply reason and judgment.

When you recognize that you have spiritual issues that interfere with your peace of mind and your relationships, half the battle is won. That awareness is the first step in your spiritual growth process.

Use the tools that follow to help you work this task. Then, as with all the tasks that follow, participants of our Spiritual Growth Group in Tucson will report on the thoughts, emotions, and actions they experienced as they worked this same task.

TOOLS FOR TASK 1

1. **Practice self-observation.** In the present moment, observe three parts of your experience:
   - Become aware of any physical sensation.
   - Sense any emotion you are feeling.
   - Observe any thought going through your head.

   Notice that different aspects of your mind can operate simultaneously.

2. **Learn to observe your own reactions with love.** Notice any judgment you make about people or events. Are your

reactions coming from the "basement" of your mind? Are the "beasts" controlling how you feel and react? Can you observe your own negative reactions with love—without condemning yourself for being weak, overly emotional, combative, fearful, etc.?

Practice observing your reactions as you would those of a child whom you love dearly. Isn't this the way your Higher Power would view you—with the acceptance, love, and wisdom of a parent or grandparent? Be kind to yourself when you self-observe.

3. **Meditate on the spiritual dimension of your life.**
Experience yourself as a spiritual being. Consider that your spiritual self includes all your thoughts and feelings. Your hopes, dreams, memories, secret urges, and driving loves are parts of what make up your spirit. Can you envision how negative thoughts and feelings work from within to attack your spiritual well-being? Can you see that the events of the external world are separate from your spiritual self?

Participants Report on Task 1

LEYLA: Within the same day I had two experiences, both while I was on the road. The first one happened when I was driving and started using my "monkey brain." I was fretting about overcommitment and why I commit to do so many things.

The monkey brain started in about how my "want to do" is bigger than my "can do," and why did I say I would do these things? I hate to back out of a commitment, but I just don't think I am going to be able to do what I promised.

I finally realized that I had traveled about two miles, not concentrating on the driving but only thinking about negatives.

Usually I don't have this type of rambling in my brain where it is just back-and-forth. I was coming from physical therapy and was in pain, so perhaps I was in a higher state of agitation. When I realized

I was deep in fear and anxiety, and insecure, and it seemed like my whole brain was collapsing, I thought, "Wait—stop! What are you doing?"

I was able to observe that my emotions were in control. I started to look around at the scenery instead. I was still driving and thinking that I did not remember seeing the last mile I had driven. Then I started taking deep breaths and calming myself. But the monkey brain came back—this time a little slower and this time I was very aware of it.

I told myself to put these thoughts aside. I said to myself, "This is a new moment in my life and I can choose differently." So I tried to be in the moment.

LEADER: Can you describe this emotion you call "monkey brain"?

I SHINED A FLASHLIGHT ON THE ANGER BEASTS IN MY BASEMENT AND THEY SCURRIED AWAY.

LEYLA: It was fear and anxiety and insecurity. It was awful. That combination for me causes this "monkey brain." It is an insistent "rat-a-tat-tat" that distracts me from what I'm doing and demands my attention.

At that moment I thought, "What a difference it makes when I am really awake and aware. I have so much control and so much power over my life and the choices I make."

BETSY: It is uncanny how, once you decide to be aware, your behavior shifts. It's like once you decide you are going to buy a new car, you notice cars.

I came home after a meeting on Friday night and my husband was making applesauce. If this had happened a year ago I would have just dropped dead with excitement that he was making applesauce. But I saw him with a red apple in his hand, and we had bought Granny

Smith apples and I had already planned to make a Waldorf salad for Sunday's church luncheon. He was using the four apples I had bought for this!

I was totally unaware. The first words out of my mouth were, "Don't use those apples! I need those apples!" Rather than saying, "This is wonderful that you are making applesauce." I could have picked many nicer responses. My first reactions were anger and frustration!

At least I was aware enough to remove myself quickly. I went and brushed my teeth and did a few other things. I was feeling so frustrated because I knew that the next day I would not have time to go out and buy what I needed for Sunday. I was like, "Why does this happen? Now what am I going to do?"

I was going through what Leyla calls monkey brain, all these negatives in the basement. What was wrong was that I didn't have the big picture. I saw that I was looking at a very narrow picture called *me*—my perspective, how things affect *me*. I realized that in a day or two this would not mean anything. It was a selfish place to be.

After thinking it through, I was able to go back to the kitchen and apologize, compliment him on making applesauce, and taste it with him. The minute I got myself in a good place, he offered to go to the store to get more apples even though it was 10 p.m. Of course I said, "No, no," and released him of any obligation.

But I notice there is a pattern with me that repeats when I'm tired. I now recognize that I am much more likely to fall into that groove of negative thinking when I'm tired.

KITTY: I have spent far too much time in the basement. This week I noticed that I had a little self-pity and self-doubt, and sometimes frustration and anger.

I have two things that have helped me enormously, and one is to stay in the moment. I find that if I stay focused in the moment and analyze the situation, I can cope a lot better. I can work toward a solution. I can stay in the proper mindset with hope and joy.

I've learned from this program that if you are all in a knot, one thing that can help is to look to the Lord and ask, "Where should I be today?" or "What can I do?" I have received strength from that. Then, if I meditate a bit, I am in better shape.

I WAS LOOKING AT A VERY NARROW PICTURE CALLED *ME.*

The most exciting thing happened as I was working this task. My son lives with me, but we are like ships in the night because he works all night. He came in from work and said, "Gee, Mom, you look better than you have in ages." Well, my first reaction was to laugh. But maybe spiritual growth is part and parcel to your health, your emotion, your appearance.

Maybe my looks reflect my ability to stay on track and keep the beasts down in their basement. It is a slow process but it is working. I think I am getting stronger through spiritual growth.

JULIE: Kitty just reminded me that I have been stewing on my awareness of what I needed to work on this past week. I realized that for my emotional health, I needed to make changes to some close relationships. I kept procrastinating because I was stewing in fear.

When I was stewing, I would become resentful. I didn't want to act from those emotions, so rather than shining a light in there, I just kept putting it off.

I found myself wondering when the next group was starting, because I felt like I was going nuts. Sure enough, we started and I saw it was about awareness. I knew already that I needed to make these changes. Now I needed to act. I was still frightened and kept going back to the resentment, trying to make it this righteous indignation I could act from.

I kept coming up with the fact that this is not where the Lord wants me to be.

I heard a song and realized that I had not been listening to music. I drive around all the time and never put the radio on. So I decided to use music to pick myself up out of the basement.

Sure enough it worked. I realized I had the strength to take action and that it was okay for me to voice what I need and what I want. I don't have to put myself at the bottom of the list; I need to be at the top of the list.

That was my major awareness: put yourself at the top of the list.

On the way here tonight, after the whole week of listening to fabulous music that made me feel more connected, I heard a lyric from the song "Tin Man" about how the Tin Man in *The Wizard of Oz* already had what the wizard gave him. On one level those words reminded me that I am always connected. Then I thought, "But what did the Tin Man do? He asked for a heart." To me that was the action. He asked the wizard for a heart and the wizard told him he already had one.

So that wrapped it up for me. You realize what you had forgotten. You remember to ask. My way of asking is praying. I had been so caught up in fear and so stuck in resentment about why I needed things to change, that the importance of changing them was buried under confusion in the basement. The music is what lifted me up out of the basement, so I am so grateful for the task this week.

BOB: Thursday morning I drove from my house to play golf. Twice on my way to the golf course people pulled out in front of me! I had to slam on my brakes to avoid a collision. It was as if they didn't want me to go to the golf course. I had anger, fear, and frustration well up inside me. It was so real to me that I could "taste" it.

The first time it happened I thought, "Okay, you are working on your spiritual growth. You can back off, take some deep breaths, and assume that guy was in a hurry to get his dog (which was in the seat beside him so he could not see me) to the vet or whatever."

But then the driver slowed down once he was in front of me, so it seemed that he was not in any hurry. It was stupid the way he was driving, and I had all these thoughts going through my mind like, "People like that should lose their license and should not be on the road!" When he turned off and out of my life, a woman in a van pulled out from a side street and made me slam on my brakes again! I was thinking, "What is going on here? What is going on in my life that I should have these risky encounters all at one time?" Of course all the fear, anxiety, and anger kind of welled up in me.

I know I must react positively to the situations in which I find myself. I shined a flashlight on the anger beasts in my basement and they scurried away. I thought that went well. I thought that this was what God wants—when I am angry, he wants me to be happy and have peace. I used some spiritual growth techniques. I am the better for it.

JACK: I had an externally guided day today, unfortunately for me. I retired in July, and the difference between my funds now and what I used to make is about $600 a month. So I thought, "Well, I'll just do some freelance work and some things I like to do. All I have to earn is $600 a month and I won't have to make any drastic cuts in lifestyle."

So I was thinking this morning that October is in the bag. But nothing is on the horizon for November. I began to stew about this. I realized I was not getting anywhere with these thoughts and that it wasn't appropriate to call anyone and beg. I had called enough times to remind them that I am still alive and well and living in Tucson and available for whatever they might have.

I thought I might as well sit down and meditate. I said a little prayer. I didn't want to pray for money—that didn't cut it—so instead I prayed for this concern I had, that no work had shown up for November. I let that go and went into the meditation. Since I had lots of time, I did a forty-five-minute meditation (I have two pieces of music and it just times out that way), and as the second piece was ending my cell phone was vibrating. I missed the call because I didn't want to abruptly end the meditation.

I called back and they had a project for Monday. Bingo—there was work. That was good. Then I went out to exercise, which I also did not really feel like doing. The phone rang again and they said they had a signing for me for the next day. They wanted me to go online and confirm I was going to do these two projects so I did that. When I opened my e-mail there was more work. I was amazed that I had said I needed $600 of work, and in the space of one meditation and one exercise session there came $150 worth of work.

AWARENESS IS THE KEY TO ALL GROWTH.
YOU MUST RECOGNIZE HOW YOU ARE REACTING.

It was one of those things where afterwards you wonder why you worried. I knew God would come through. Every time something like that happens, it's a reminder to me that if I had a little more faith I would be a lot more comfortable.

TAMI: While working this task, I was very aware that I had issues every day. I had all these negative thoughts in my mind. I wonder if it's because I am tired and overwhelmed. Is it because I am stressed and have added responsibilities? Is this something I chose? Is this what life has dealt me? Is it because I am actually a negative person?

Earlier today I was overwhelmed with negativity to the point where I called a friend while driving. It was monkey brain like Leyla says; I never had a name for that but that is what it was. In my mind, I kept trying to recall the task but was so engrossed with this over-whelming sensation of sadness mixed with helplessness.

My sister had called me that morning; her father-in-law had passed away. I had envy that he got to go and I did not. I was mad at myself at that moment and I hated looking at all this negative stuff in this situation.

I have so many more issues and problems pounding at my door, I cannot list them all. As far as the house model goes, I have risen above that basement for sure. I was actually at the top of that roof, ready to jump! I wasn't in the basement—I wanted to go on the roof and jump, hoping to fly or that God would catch me. Then I thought, "Well, I could probably end up right back in that basement or maybe at the top of the stairs if I did jump." I just wanted to get away from it all.

I called my friend because I had to turn to someone. She is very spiritual and knows how to pray. I hoped she could help me refocus. I thought, "Heck with shining the flashlight; I cannot even *find* the flashlight!" As I was bellowing to my friend over my dilemma and giving her a crash lesson about this spiritual growth course, and how I am supposed to look at negativity in my mind but that she sprung into my thoughts . . . what do I do when I can't even sort my thoughts surrounding all these emotions?

Then it occurred to me, like the morning sun peaking over the mountain with a moment of clarity, that "This too shall pass." It is not right before the sun comes up. It is right *when* the sun pops up, that I experience that moment of truth.

You know it is a process. Even though you don't like what is happening, it is the right thing that is happening at the right time. This comes to you all at once as if you just know it. I had to relinquish my feelings and give up to God the idea that we are in control. We need to allow God to do his work by getting out of the way.

In a moment, I recognized the fear. I could not remember what the task was about, other than negative emotions. I did not want to deal with negative emotions, but when it occurred to me that God is still in control, even through the storms—like when the sun is shining while it rains—I could find strength and move forward.

This is not giving in to negative emotions, but it is recognizing the negativity. Like the task suggests: first we need to know where we are in order to know where to go. This is why we must look at ourselves and know where our negative emotions lie. Observe our emotions as they are occurring in order to practice refocusing our negative thoughts.

MICHAEL: I had a blood draw appointment scheduled for ten thirty this morning. I was sitting there and noticed some people were going ahead of me. I had that instant reaction of anger, abandonment, "what a screwed-up operation." The thoughts went really fast, but I took a breath to release them. I said to the person at the desk, "I think I have been lost in the shuffle." I remained calm.

Suddenly there was an office manager and two clerks and people running around looking for me because they had lost me in the shuffle. Finally a person came up and smiled, saying, "I am taking your record personally to where it needs to go." Moments later I was in and quickly out. I know it was a matter of taking that breath and being there and letting it flow.

LEADER: There is very little a session leader can add to those wonderful reports on becoming aware. But remember, as we discussed last week, awareness is the key to all growth. You must know what you are experiencing. You must recognize how you are reacting to the negative. And then you must deal with that reaction, whether that means shining a little bitty flashlight on the "beast" or, like Tami, using the entire light of the sun to illuminate your issues.

Enrichment Reading

1. In its own right, or apart from spiritual life, earthly life is nothing but sleep. But an earthly life that has spiritual life within it is wide awake. (Emanuel Swedenborg, *Revelation Unveiled* 158)

2. People who have not been regenerated are dreaming; people who have been regenerated are awake. In fact, in the Word our earthly life is compared to a sleep and our spiritual life to wakefulness. (Emanuel Swedenborg, *True Christianity* 606)

3. Everything good and true comes from the Lord and everything evil and false from hell. If people believed in this, the true situation, they could not be charged with any failing or have evil ascribed to them. (Emanuel Swedenborg, *Secrets of Heaven* 6324)

4. Keep awake, therefore, for you do not know on what day your Lord is coming. But understand this: if the owner of the house had known in what part of the night the thief was coming, he would have stayed awake and would not have let his house be broken into. (Matthew 24:42,43)

Task 2

RAISE YOUR MIND

 Once a day, practice raising your mind to a higher level.

- You can use this task to deal with a negative emotion—to rise above anger, fear, resentment, etc.
- You can practice this task in relation to another person—raising your mind to see him or her from an angelic point of view.
- You may use this task in relation to religious study or contemplation of nature, elevating your mind to see scripture or nature in the light of heaven. What is the message here from your Higher Power?
- You might use this task in relation to a particular event or circumstance in your life. How does that event or situation look in relation to your eternal life story?

Learning Objectives
- *After awareness, move to a higher place in your mind.*
- *Learn to view events from the perspective of a Higher Power.*

We have each been given an amazing ability to focus our attention on any one of many different mental levels. A lot of people go through life never realizing that there are levels in the mind and that you can move up and down between those levels.

We pay a high price for not knowing this. For example, every negative emotion depends on you being in the lowest level. As soon as you get out of the lowest level, that negative emotion loses its power. That is one reason people are unaware of the higher levels: it is as if the negative emotion has an investment in you being asleep or unaware of something else you can access. It wants control!

So imagine you are terrified of some situation and are caught up in imagining, "Well what if this, and what if that?" and "The world is going to come to an end." These thoughts all support the whirlwind of the negative emotion.

But if you move up just a little higher and look at things from that new point of view, you would see how unfounded those fears are and how much they depend on illusion. You might gain a different perspective that makes a huge difference to your spiritual life.

I am going to give you my Mountaintop Sermon. It is one of the shortest sermons I have ever given. It usually requires an hour of driving and an hour of hiking before I get to it. Since we don't have that much time, I invite you to climb mentally with me to the top of Mount Lemmon, the highest peak of the Santa Catalina Mountains in Arizona.

Looking out over the vast valley below, you can see the distant Santa Rita Mountains to the south and the Rincons to our left. You can see the Tucson Mountains to our right and the huge valley in between. There are a half a million people in the valley.

There are people going to work; there are people coming home from work; there are people who are upset because the traffic light turned red. There are people who were just involved in an accident. There are people in the hospital and people in the emergency room. There are people being born and people dying. There are people making love and people making war. There are people who are terrified and people who are peaceful.

But what does it look like from this vantage point? It is one perfect harmony. Everything is beautiful and as it should be.

You see, from God's point of view, the world is going along fine. The closer you get to the level on which people live, the more you can get caught up in little things like the way we live and die over traffic (for one example). As if they matter in the grander scheme of things.

It is like the father watching his child play at the beach. The child builds a sand castle and the waves come in and destroy the castle. The child's world comes to an end. Does the father cry? No, he smiles, because he has a higher vantage point and he sees this little event as part of the grander picture; he doesn't get caught up in the small picture.

In any situation, we can access the higher level and view it differently. I have known people who do this as they go in for surgery. You might think, "This is terrible, they are about to go under the knife and their heart might stop during the operation, or something else terrible might happen." Yet you find the patient in a very peaceful state. I think sometimes we are given the ability to access our peaceful levels at the very moment when we need peace most.

Sometimes people going into battle get into a state of peace. We can get caught up in the illusion that we must be upset because of the situation, but the situation does not cause the upset. What causes the upset is that we are stuck in the basement and we need to get to a higher level to interpret our situation properly.

Viewing our situation from the highest level enables us to see our life as far out as eternity. Five minutes or five years or one hundred years are as nothing compared to eternity. So if you are really upset about something, just access the higher level and think, "I wonder how this looks in relation to my eternal welfare."

While I was waiting for our group's meeting to begin, I found myself standing outside wanting cars to come in the parking lot. And then I thought, "This is crazy, let's go to the higher level." On the higher level, you can see all the cars. They have already left home and the people are in the cars, converging on this place. Because I had not seen that, I had the emotion going, "Are they coming or aren't they?" But it was already in the cards, wasn't it? So that emotion depends on me having a very limited point of view. I can make up stuff to be upset about. The ego always likes to be upset.

There are other things we can achieve by raising the mind. One of them is to see more deeply and understand things that are otherwise an enigma. Swedenborg tells a story where he was talking to an angel in the spiritual world and the angel challenged his view of the Trinity, and Swedenborg said, "Go deeper into my thinking, please, and you may perhaps find some agreement" (*Revelation Unveiled* 961).

Have you ever had the thought that disagreements depend on a failure to understand the other person's point of view, and that if you really understood another person, you would agree with them? How can you understand another person's point of view? You must rise to a higher level and be willing to look at it from a more universal plane or perspective.

TOOLS FOR TASK 2

1. **Try the higher viewpoint.** Close your eyes and remember a moment that disturbed you this week. Identify the emotion you felt at that moment. It could have been anger, fear, jealousy, or any of the "beasts" that dwell in the basement of your mind. Now imagine that you are magically viewing that same disturbance from a high point such as a mountaintop, an airplane window, or

atop a tall building. Notice that from this lofty view all is quiet and peaceful—that the irritation cannot reach your mind or spirit at this higher level.

Is the negative emotion weakened by your higher view?

2. **Apply the Five-Year Rule.** Think of a negative event that destroyed your happiness this past week. Now place that negative event in a much longer time perspective. For example, imagine yourself five years from now, and ask yourself:

   - Will I remember this event in five years?
   - Will its power to destroy my happiness still have any strength?

   Does this longer perspective reduce its power over me right now?

Participants Report on Task 2

HERB: The habit I have carried with me from many spiritual growth sessions is that when I get up in the morning, I greet the Lord. Then I recite the Serenity Prayer. A short prayer follows me all day. If I have a little problem, it pops into my mind.

But I do have one big problem that has been bothering me for a couple of months now. My daughter was diagnosed with lung cancer. First I got angry. She smoked for fifty years and for more than thirty years I tried to get her to stop.

I also had fear because I know about cancer. I have had two bouts of cancer myself and the good Lord pulled me through. I also remembered that you can't do it without prayer.

When I had cancer, many people put me on their prayer list. I have a nephew who belongs to Nazarene Church, and he had churches around the country put me on their prayer lists.

My daughter is on those prayer lists. But every day I get angry! The fact is that she brought it on herself. I tried to guide her and it didn't work. She is a mother of six and a grandmother of twenty-one. She has done a beautiful job with her life, so that is fine.

And now, the tumor is gone! There is no presence of cancer anywhere else in her body. She is taking tests and finishing up chemotherapy to try to get rid of it altogether.

LEADER: That is wonderful, Herb. So you raised yourself above the anger and let the love for your daughter take over again? Prayer is one way of raising your thoughts.

HERB: That's right.

I WOKE UP THIS MORNING STILL BURNING WITH IT. WHAT I NEEDED WAS THAT VIEW FROM MOUNT LEMMON.

LEYLA: The Serenity Prayer goes through my mind often, even with small everyday things.

This week, I phoned in two prescription refills to my pharmacy. This used to be simple, when they had an automated system where you press a number to talk to the pharmacist. Their new system connects you to a phone bank overseas, so you cannot talk to anyone in the pharmacy.

When I saw that one of my refills would need a doctor's permission, I called to check the status; the system said one was ready but the other had a problem with insurance. So I called back and maneuvered through the phone bank. The service rep then transferred me to the insurance department. I could hear that I had been transferred but no one would speak. So I called back and started over, but the phone bank people had limited information so I hung up. Fifteen minutes later I got an automated call from the pharmacy, saying one prescription was ready and my insurance would not pay for the other. So I called my doctor's office (which the pharmacy used to do for me) and they said they would take care of it.

When I went to the pharmacy to get this prescription, I talked to them about their new phone system. They weren't happy either! They said they liked it the old way.

I was frustrated and angry, but I had to accept what was. I raised my awareness to a level of just accepting. I should be quicker to do this.

I know I have a choice. I can't do the same thing over and over and expect different results. I am going to take my prescriptions away from this company; that is all I can do.

LEADER: Leyla, which beasts grabbed you and pulled you into that basement?

LEYLA: Frustration. Anger.

LEADER: They are very strong, aren't they? They can pull you down to a lower level anytime they want.

LEYLA: Yes!

KITTY: Raising your mind is hard in tough times. My son transferred into the spiritual world, and there is a key word: "accept." I have difficulty accepting. It is not like he is sending me e-mail or stuff like that!

I am developing an understanding, and Swedenborg's writings are helpful. I trust that there is a spiritual world and my son is part of it. This is like raising my mind and accepting more without needing tangible proof, like a return message that assures me: "Are you okay, Andy?" "Yes I'm fine, Mom."

I am trying to accept more and raise my mind to a spiritual level. It was a good task for me this week and one that I am going to have to repeat until I get it right. I am doing much better by believing and having faith that there is a spiritual world. It is a big step for me.

JACK: I was able to use this task with really good effect this morning. I got into a nasty e-mail exchange with somebody who I won't see face-to-face until tomorrow.

In my view, what happened was that I was asked for input on an idea and I said I did not like the idea. He then said I did not have the authority to have an opinion, and he enumerated why. That really upset me. I was ready for a screaming confrontation with this individual. Then I thought, you know, this started as an e-mail "beast" and it has gone about as far as it dares.

I woke up this morning about 4 a.m. still burning with it. When I did get up, I had my MP3 that has two ten-minute meditations followed by music. So this morning I did the twenty-minute meditation, and thought what I needed was that view from Mount Lemmon.

For several hours I got real relief. I went about doing other things and not paying any attention to this beast that was nagging at me. Now, as tomorrow approaches, and the in-person confrontation looms, it is a little harder. I can feel myself being dragged back into the basement with all kinds of "what ifs?"

At any rate, it worked wonderfully this morning. If I have trouble going to sleep tonight, I intend to meditate again and try to get the view from Mount Lemmon.

GRATITUDE IS WHAT GOT ME OUT OF IT.

LEADER: Thanks, Jack. Yes, meditation is a great help in raising our minds to a heavenly plane, where we can view a situation from a perspective of peace and love.

BETSY: I had a few opportunities to work this task. I found that gratitude was the changing factor that got me up onto a higher plane, where I could see what was happening from a better viewpoint. I have two instances to report.

One sounds so trivial after listening to the others' reports. I attended a wedding. It was a family that my family is close to. My kids were invited to the wedding but it looked like none of them were coming. I had done my motherly thing by suggesting several times that they attend.

I got there and saw all these people that they knew and had connections with. So I called two of them and said, "Can't you come?"

What was happening was that I was really disappointed that they were not there. Then I became judgmental that they did not make the effort or take the time. Here I was in the midst of all those great people, and it was a pity they weren't there too.

Gratitude is what got me out of it. Gratitude in the present moment and not thinking I had the right to control any of it, was really helpful for me. It turned out that one of my children did come and loved it. So it worked out.

The second instance was on Halloween. Our son and his girlfriend were coming for dinner. I was on my feet all day getting ready for this. About an hour before they came, I realized I was *really* tired. I was just bone tired and could have gone to bed right then. I thought, how am I going to get through this? I wanted to be in a good place and loved the fact that they were coming over. But I was feeling frustration and self-pity, and a little fear because I was hurting.

Again, gratitude is what got me through. I told myself that the universe is not limited on energy. Those adorable kids coming to the door for "trick or treat" will give me energy.

Sure enough that is exactly what happened. Our son and his girlfriend came dressed in unbelievable costumes, and the whole thing just worked out. It is a leap of faith—I have had so many experiences where, when I elevate my mind and give it a chance, it always turns out better. I just have to remember this before I decide not to do something.

LEADER: Thanks, Betsy. You mentioned that these "opportunities" to work the task were "small things." I find that it is an accumulation of small things that most often drags me down into my basement. I'm thankful when I can take the present moment to raise myself above the little annoyances and be grateful for the big picture.

VICKY: I had a very challenging week. I lost my sister this summer, so I'm trying to deal with that. Going through her things and sorting them has been very hard. I had one really rough day when I was trying to get her car cleaned so we could put it up for sale.

My husband had gone to work, and he had put the handbrake on so hard I could not release it and take the car to the car wash. I was exasperated and could not get my bearings. I could not put my feet on the ground.

Finally I just sat down and thought, "This has got to stop! I can't do this." I thought about what I could do. I remembered that when you are in the midst of everything you forget what you have learned.

What worked for me was writing. Through the years I have done it off and on. I thought I would start again. I have been doing some morning journaling, and the rest of the week has gone pretty well. I start my morning pages and instead of just writing, I say "Good morning, God," and just pour it all out. By the time I am done sifting through that, I can get down to gratitude and the blessings I do have.

I remembered what Tami said last week. I looked up and the sun was really bright. I knew it was going to be a good day, and I could end my writing with a couple of affirmations that I can repeat during the day to keep myself grounded and centered.

TAMI: Friday afternoon, I have all my work finished and I am all set to leave the office by 5 p.m. I am anxious to beat the traffic and get through the road construction in front of the building.

It is hard to live in the moment when I'm thinking about going to the beaches of Mexico. I should be there by 10 p.m. and can already picture the water by the moonlight. I close my eyes and can almost feel the cool ocean breeze and smell the saltwater as I take a deep breath.

But, when I open my eyes, I am disappointed to see a coworker coming into the office. He wants to get client files and information off the computer.

I remember this week's task—Raise Your Mind. I let him know of my excitement for the weekend and my hopes to leave at 5 p.m.

As we start to download the files, my personal phone rings with a ringtone that lets me know it's the person I'm meeting to drive to Mexico. She is probably on the way to meet me. I will call when I leave. Then a different ringtone signals that my son is calling. I am still working on the computer. I remember the task. My coworker is a pleasant person. I have only met him twice, but he keeps asking me these questions I cannot answer.

I am reminded that I am going to leave in fifteen minutes. We are almost finished, and surprisingly I am not as nervous or anxious as I expected to be when I first saw him approaching. This week's task seems to be working.

I get through the traffic. It is a beautiful sunset. I fill up my gas tank and am waiting for my friend. I am working the task! Hey, it is pretty easy so far. We are off on the road to Mexico! Not much traffic at all. At the Mexico border, the American border patrol has traffic lined up. It is 9 p.m. I work the task again. Waiting behind these trucks and trailers lined up with cargo. We slide through the inspection with a few questions from border patrol and no waiting, with a green light on the Mexican side. There is no stopping us now. The ocean is less than an hour away!

We make it to the gate near the beach house and let the guard know where we are going to stay. He motions us straight ahead.

But straight ahead takes us to the off-beaten side road. We get stuck in the sand as the back tire of my new Toyota truck spins; the rear differential lock system is activated, but instead of getting us out of the sand, it only buries the back wheels deeper.

The guards come with shovels and, after an hour of digging, we're still stuck. Now how does one rise above this? I get the camera out to capture the moment, and my friend says, "Put the camera away. I will remember it in my mind. I don't need a picture!"

She keeps asking if we'll be able to get out. It is a good time to work the task again, and a great reminder that the task is never really finished; it is a continuum of our spiritual growth.

My new Mexican friends go to get four more friends with another Toyota truck. They all stand behind my pickup after letting air out of the tires, and pull us to solid ground. We follow them to our destination and wave *adiós*.

It was well after midnight when we finally arrived, but the ocean seemed the most beautiful I had ever seen in the moonlight. And it was kind of interesting because I was in happy mode. I really needed to work this task, and it helped.

MICHAEL: I found this task difficult. My mind wanders.

We are flying over El Paso at thirty-three thousand feet on the way to Dallas, and I am "looking down from above." It looks peaceful. The sunlight is glinting off the buildings. That is how I picture looking down from a higher point of view; I see myself up above, looking down on a scene. That's when I started making associations.

There was Biggs Air Force Base where I might have been assigned many years ago, and I thought how that would have changed my life. There was Interstate 10, where we traveled when we moved from Philadelphia to Tucson in 1990. From those associations my mind descended to what was happening on the ground—all the drugs, all the killings, all the border problems.

From above it looks great and peaceful. But on the ground it is the rough and tumble of daily living. When I get thinking about that, I get thinking about my anger about politics in this country, the wars around the world, violence, and all that stuff. It is toxic for me. So the way out, using the process of thinking from above, is trying to get back from the rough and tumble to that "place above" to avoid the toxic situations in my life.

I am getting better at that, and I try daily to find a way to connect with that inner serenity. I like finding a person to talk to who listens to my mind or my spirit. That connection automatically takes me to a higher place. That is the place I like to be all the time.

BOB: Like you, Michael, I had a terrible time with this task. I recognized that I needed to raise my mind when I started whining to myself. I was whining about the fact that I sometimes cannot keep up with these young guys that I play tennis and golf with. To be honest, my ego is so deeply involved with that aspect of my social life. That is partly because I did not have the chance to participate in social sports much as a kid. I had to work my way through high school and through college.

I participated in some sports but not nearly as much as I would have liked to. Later on, in two careers, I was a workaholic. Any free time I had I tried to spend with the family and not at the golf course or with the guys. I don't regret that at all—it's just that when I did retire and had the time to do social sports, it became a very important part of my life, and how I act and perform in that part of my life became an ego-driven thing.

You can see I have bangs all over me because one of the young guys I play with took me out like a fullback on the tennis court on Saturday. He was my partner and he did not think I was going to get to a ball. I had set up to hit a backhand with my back turned, and the next thing I know I'm rolling across the tennis court. I can show you my bruises!

The point I am trying to make is that I started to feel a degree of depression about the fact that I have inadequacies in the social sports part of my life. I feel jealousy because I want to be back at my peak. I need to realize that my peak is past, and this is difficult to deal with at this point in my life.

Once I realized it was an ego-driven thing, I asked, "How do I raise myself to a higher viewpoint?" I needed to see where this fits into my life by looking at it from a higher level.

I saw that sports are an important part of my social life, whether I win or lose. As long as I can maintain an attitude that keeps me fun to play with, I will have a social life, and that is important. The guys don't seem to mind beating up on me—it is retribution for me having beaten up on them in years past.

IT IS AN ACCUMULATION OF SMALL THINGS THAT MOST OFTEN DRAGS ME DOWN INTO MY BASEMENT.

I also realized that if I back off from sports, it would be like wanting to run away and escape. I could see, looking at it from a higher perspective, that this would create a void in my life.

As God often does for me, he sent a message. This one came in an e-mail—I don't know who sent it; it could have been one of hundreds of people. What this e-mail said, when I was trying to rise above these feelings of inadequacy and depression, was that being happy is not about being perfect. Being happy is about deciding to see beyond your imperfections.

Out of the clear blue sky this thing came! It was such a meaningful message to me, and it helped me rise above those feelings of inadequacy and depression. So far, I think I can live with "less than perfect." I can do it; I know I can. So my work is to rise above it. I also need to remember that I was *never* "perfect"! I realize that this feeling of inadequacy is just one of the beasts in my basement that wants me to come down to its level.

LEADER: This is a lifelong task. Raising your mind to get a better and more accurate perspective on what is bothering you helps bring peace and happiness. Things seem much more serene when viewed from the mountaintop.

Enrichment Reading

1. To you, O Lord, I lift up my soul. (Psalms 25:1)

2. I lift up my eyes to the hills—from where will my help come? My help comes from the Lord, who made heaven and earth. (Psalms 121:1,2)

3. Teach me the way I should go, for to you I lift up my soul. (Psalms 143:8)

4. We have become so superficial that we are unwilling to give credence to anything but what is physical. This gratifies our love and therefore gratifies our discernment; so we are uncomfortable raising our thoughts above the physical level toward anything spiritual separated from what is physical. (Emanuel Swedenborg, *Divine Love and Wisdom* 374)

5. From birth, all we love is ourselves and the world, because this is all that comes into our view. So this is all we think about. . . . This love cannot be separated from its impurity unless we have the ability to lift our discernment into heaven's light and see how we need to live in order to have our love raised up into wisdom along with our discernment. It is through discernment that our love sees—that we, in fact, see—which evils are defiling and polluting our love. This also enables us to see that if we resolutely abstain from those evils as sins, we love the opposites of those evils, which are all heavenly. . . . Love sees all this—that is, we see all this—by using our ability to lift our discernment into heaven's light, which gives us wisdom. Then to the extent that love puts heaven first and the world second, at the same time putting the Lord first and ourselves second, love is cleansed of

its pollutants and purified. That is, it is to that extent lifted into heaven's warmth and united to the light of heaven that surrounds discernment. Then the marriage takes place that is called the marriage of the good and the true, the marriage of love and wisdom.... This illustrates the truth that love or volition is cleansed in our discernment if they are raised up together. (Emanuel Swedenborg, *Divine Love and Wisdom* 419)

Task 3

STOP TAKING CREDIT

 Observe your lower nature trying to take credit for what you say and do.

- You may notice resentment in your lower nature because you are not getting sufficient recognition or praise.

- You may observe a certain pleasure and self-satisfaction when you are praised.

- When you become conscious of one of these states, say in your heart: "This praise does not belong to me. Give God the praise." Then observe any change in yourself.

Learning Objectives

- *Experience the negative emotion when credit due is not given.*

- *Understand that good comes from our Higher Power and not from within us.*

- *Notice your reaction to praise, and in what part of the "house" your reaction resides.*

One interesting thing about the ego is how it likes to swell with pride. Have you ever been in the situation where someone looks at you and says something like, "You have beautiful eyes," and you think, "Wow!"—as if you deserved credit for the compliment?

It tickles me when someone comes up to me and says, "You are the spitting image of my Uncle Fred"—and you may be thinking, "Now, his Uncle Fred might be ugly," but somehow I swell with pride that I look just like his Uncle Fred. The ego wants to take credit for everything. It is amazing the greed it has.

One symptom of the ego's greed is its feeling that it is not acknowledged enough. But if my hand picks up my glasses, do I think, "Thank you, hand, for picking up the glasses." Suppose my hand wanted to take credit for everything it did?

One day I was painting a picture and someone said, "You did a beautiful job." If the hand said, "What about me? I did all the work!" I would have to say, "No, hand, it was not you, it was the arm. Without the arm you could not work." So the arm would swell with pride and I would have to tell it that without the brain it could not operate. And without the love of painting, the brain could not operate. Where does the credit go? Who does the work of art?

Suppose you do a good deed for your neighbor and the neighbor says, "That was so charitable of you. You are such a loving, wonderful person." And your ego starts to swell with pride. But there is something inappropriate about that reaction.

Now suppose a person says, "It wasn't me; it was God who did it." How do you react?

The reality is that all good is done by our Higher Power, through people. Our Higher Power gives the lower orders of creation the feeling that we are doing good, and we get to have this wonderful sense of participation.

There is a wonderful parable in the New Testament in which Jesus talks about the master and the servant. When the servant comes in to eat, the master says, "Feed me first and then feed yourself." So the servant feeds the master. Jesus says, "Does the master thank the servant because he did what he was supposed to do? So likewise you, when you have done all these things which are commanded say, 'We are servants and we have done that which was our duty to do.'"

How can you take credit for doing anything in your life? Does this question ring true for you, or does it leave something left out? Aren't we supposed to thank one another? How do you feel when people thank you? You feel like they appreciated what you did, right?

What if they leaned on you and said, "You don't really get it—I am thanking you because you did a wonderful thing here." Don't let it throw you off balance when people thank you too much; we know in our hearts that what we do is so little.

I have had the pleasure of going to the opera. Suppose someone in the opera said, "I want to thank you for going to the opera. It was so good of you to go to the opera." I would say, "Now wait a minute, I did not go to the opera to get brownie points; I went to the opera to enjoy it."

If you were to thank an angel profusely for living a good life and doing so many useful things, the angel would feel uncomfortable. "I am not doing it to get credit. I am doing it because I love to do it and it is not me doing it anyway, the Lord does it. I am just the instrument." It is like thanking the trumpet for the concerto. Sometimes I feel like a trumpet in the Lord's hands; sometimes battered and beaten and dented, but every now and then some music comes through.

If you applaud Russian performers, they applaud back to you. Why? Have you ever been in the position where you have done something and you have felt like clapping? There are many things involved, but one is gratitude that other people want to come and hear you sing. For me I know it is gratitude that I can sing, or paint, or whatever it is.

The ego has an insatiable appetite for praise and glory. I find it is an interesting challenge to not get caught up in this thought that "I deserve this" or "What do I get out of this?" or "Am I getting enough praise?" These are the things the ego demands.

What is the opposite of taking credit? It is taking blame. Now consider a related emotion: the fear of being blamed. Instead of craving credit, the ego fears blame and criticism. Consider the person who is afraid to talk in public because he will feel so ashamed if he does a bad job of it. What is the assumption behind that? Somehow he is supposed to be brilliant, and if he's not brilliant people will not like him.

Both sides of this emotional coin—pride and fear of criticism—can cripple our ability to gracefully accept gratitude and criticism. In reality, it is simply a privilege to be alive and a privilege to serve.

The musician plays music from a love of doing it. In my own life, I got started on some of the good things I did because I wanted praise and glory. Later, I realized that I did those things because they were useful to others. In the spiritual sense, you find after a while that you do something for someone because you love to do it—which means you are shifting to a higher level where the love of doing good is more powerful than the love of being rewarded for doing it.

So the task this week is to look at the ways in which our greedy ego tries to take credit for things, and at how you react when you feel you are not getting enough credit or when you fear blame.

TOOLS FOR TASK 3

1. **Observe your reactions when you are not given the credit you feel you deserve.**

   Think about a time when your hard work was not recognized by others or rewarded with gratitude. What emotions came up from your basement? Did you feel injured or slighted? Notice if you have a love for praise as a reward. Can you replace it with gratitude for the opportunity to serve?

2. **Examine your reactions to blame—the opposite of praise.**

   How have you felt when you were unfairly blamed for a failure or oversight? Which of your "beasts" tried to take control of your reactions? Did anger, fear, or jealously enter your mind and drag you down?

3. **Remember your reactions when you were praised.**

   Recall a time when you received praise. Did you swell with pride? Did that pride make you forget how others contributed to your success? Do you often like to take full credit for good work? Take a moment now to let go of credit, and thank your Higher Power for the goodness that flows through you.

Participants Report on Task 3

HERB: As I look back on my life when I was a young soldier, I see that if I didn't get praise, I felt useless. If I did get praise, I was on top of the world.

One of those experiences bothered me for a long time. I was telling my company commander all the things I had done in my career. He listened and when I was done he said, "Sergeant, I don't care what you have done. What counts is what you are going to do while you are here." I was hurt and I had a heck of a time getting out of the funk it created. I guess my ego was really bruised!

About five years ago I had double bypass surgery and was finishing rehab when I ran into the doctor who did the surgery. I had never met him except right before the surgery. I thanked him very much for what he had done. And he said, "Don't thank me, thank God for giving me the talent to do these procedures." That caused me to think about the humility of some people who do great things.

He took my thanks as praise and passed it on to God. I have learned over the years that I don't need praise. I generally want to have things to do. I set my goals and if I can reach them, that is great with me. If someone wants to praise me, that is fine. I don't need it if I have done what I think I should do.

LEADER: It sounds to me as if the younger Herb could be put in the basement very quickly. He lived there by being put down or not receiving praise that he thought he deserved. I think that most of us, when we were younger, were more sensitive to that.

TRACY: It was interesting to start the task doing what I was doing at the time, conducting training. At the end of every training session I always have to do trainer evaluations. I have lived in that modality for the last twenty-six years. It bothers me that I even care about the evaluations, but on the basis of the evaluations being good, I get the next job.

I tried to look at the evaluations last week and realized that someone had given me the absolute worst evaluation I have ever had! I just wanted to put this behind me and was able to let it go.

Part of what I was processing was that everything I have done for a long time has been to push other people forward and help them achieve their goals. I help them do what they want to do. I have been sorting that out in my mind. The real question for me was: "When can I do what *I* want to do?"

So just before this task I decided I would speak up and say I wanted to do these things for myself now. But I am still working on behalf of other people. Rather than speaking out this week and saying, "No, I don't want to do that," I just found myself being quiet and not taking credit for the work I had done.

That made me realize that I was consciously not asking for credit or taking credit for any of these other things I do. How very frequently I want that! This was the stunning part of the task for me. I learned that it can be anywhere from little things like, "Did you like the breakfast I made?" to bigger things like, "How did you like the advertisement that I wrote?"

This task is going to be ongoing for me, because I realized that while I like working in the background, I have this program in my head that says, "Pat me on the head." So I have been reminding myself that it is not about me, it is about God. I am doing God's work and God's service. I am not there yet, but this is a good task.

WHEN THEY DID TOO MUCH TO ACKNOWLEDGE ME, I DIDN'T KNOW WHAT TO FEEL.

BOB: My report back surprised me because I was in an informal environment where a new acquaintance was sitting with some old friends of mine and, by way of conversation, one of my old friends said, "Bob is a genius! He can do anything. He can fix computers. He put his own air conditioner in. He can fix cars and does work on all kinds of things."

My reaction was embarrassment. I thought I was an individual who needed praise. I know I did when I was younger. But this was too much!

Now, all of a sudden I was embarrassed. I caught myself blushing. What surprised me was that I was taken aback by this rather than accepting of it. It was too lavish praise from someone who did not know me that well. I appreciated the high opinion that my friend holds of me, but I felt like it wasn't deserved and I had another feeling come over me: "I hope he doesn't call me for help on these things."

I didn't even have a chance to say I didn't feel I deserved the praise. I never thought to take the next step and say that if I had talent it was only that my Higher Power gave me that talent. I wish I had said that I am using that talent to be useful to others around me. I never got that far because I was flustered by how blatant this praise was. My ego was eating it up. The beast was well fed that day.

Didn't we say that sometime during the week our Higher Power would make an opportunity to work this task even if we didn't think we would get any praise? It happened to me. I have a ways to go with this task. The ego is far too greedy!

VICKY: Usually I like to do things without a lot of recognition and be low-key about everything. But I had been asked to do a lot of sewing for the church, and they had a big luncheon where they recognized a lot of people.

I was part of one group that got recognized, but on the way home I thought about how all the sewing and the stress I had over it did not get mentioned. Then I thought to myself, "Why do I care?" So that was an interesting feeling.

The next day at church I felt embarrassed because I got called to come up to the front and be acknowledged for all the work I had done. I was given flowers! I was blown out of the water. I just wanted to be invisible. It was really strange because I had felt sorry for myself that no one had noticed, and then, when they did too much to acknowledge me, I didn't know what to feel.

LEADER: That is wonderful. It is amazing how we react to different stimuli in our life, isn't it?

MICHAEL: Not taking credit and taking credit—this is an easy task for me. Three times I was complimented for what a great job I was doing on projects that I was working on. I said thank you and totally agreed that I did deserve the credit.

I have learned over the years that when someone compliments me, I'm not to hem and haw but to simply say "Thank you" and move on. The hard part was praise. Immediately I start thinking about the praises: "Praise the Lord" and "All glory, praise, and honor to the eternal King."

For me there is good praise and there is bad praise. The good praise is when someone says, "Michael, you did a great job." And I reply that we are all in this together. And I really feel that connection. It is not me up here and you down there; it is that we are all in this together. I am but an instrument, a vessel through which the energy flows to accomplish the task. I really feel that.

WHEN PEOPLE PRAISE ME, MY RESPONSE IS THAT I AM JUST DOING WHAT I DO.

Bad praise is when that little voice says, "Yeah, you are really good but people did not say enough to make me feel that." I thrive on positive feedback about what a great group I had just led. Sometimes I don't think I get enough!

There is also the bad praise of passive-aggressiveness—I am not quite sure how that works but it is something like, "You should have been more praising of what I did." Today, I know that the praise belongs to the Creator who made me and that it is okay to acknowledge my own accomplishments.

LEADER: Julie, before you start I would like to praise you for the way you took the initiative to use our e-mail group and respond that night that you were flooded and couldn't make our meeting. It was meaningful. I was going to contact you to ask if I could share it with the whole group but when I got back there was a second e-mail waiting for me that you had already done it. Thank you. That is a lesson for all of us that if you are not going to be here, if you want to write a few things to share with everyone, just pass it along to the group via e-mail.

JULIE: You are welcome. Up to this point in my life, when people praise me, my response is that I am just doing what I do. In the back of my mind is that God is the one who gave me the talent to do whatever it is I am doing. I don't say that aloud, I just say that I am doing what I do. Sometimes I use phrases like, "God put me here to do this." On one hand that is acknowledging the Lord and not taking credit.

I SEE PRAISE AS A GOOD THING IF . . . YOU CAN SAY, "OKAY, I DID IT, BUT I KNOW I DID NOT DO IT ON MY OWN."

My challenge that keeps coming back this week has to do with raising my two nieces. I have custody because of drug problems on their side of the family. There were certainly times when I look at their side of the family and think, "I am up here and you are down there, and that is why I am taking care of them and you can't see them!" I have had to make a lot of hard decisions about if and when they are allowed to see them. I have seldom allowed it.

About six months ago, I allowed the mother back into their lives. It has been difficult for me. On one level, people tell me all the time that I am doing a good job. My response is that I am just doing what I do and that God put me here to do this.

I want to start saying that more out loud; that is what this task has brought to me. I also noticed that when I get praise, I get very teary. I realized throughout this week that this is God saying that it is him doing this.

Last night, I got an e-mail from the grandparents saying that they wanted to see the girls tomorrow. I started out with the usual, "I am up here, you are down there." But I had to look at what has been going on through the year. The mom is seeing them now, so I thought I should let the grandparents see them too. I had told them that, unless the mother is involved, I didn't think it was fair to the young children for them to be involved.

I felt that I had to step back and review my actions. I know that I had hurt their hearts. I realized that I could now make the decision to allow a visit. I could begin the healing process.

I believed that my decision was good, but I also knew that I might have caused all their pain. It was really hard for me. I never thought all those feelings would come up with doing this task.

When I noticed that the grandparents were due in a half hour, I started weeping. But this time I was feeling God telling me, "You didn't cause this. You have been strong. I will guide you. You are the vessel full of love for those little girls."

That was such a relief. They were grateful for the visit and it was a good feeling. I kept coming back to the knowledge that the Lord is guiding me but I have to take action. Otherwise things might not be safe.

LEADER: I think you've provided a great example of that part of our enrichment reading where Emanuel Swedenborg talks about false merit and evil in *Heaven and Hell*. If we can attribute the good to God, as the inflow from God for which we are a vessel, we also have to attribute all those negative beasts as inflow from evil. You had to deal with weeping from joy and also concern from negative thoughts that were coming through. It sounds to me like you balanced them well.

JACK: I liked your story, Vicky. There was something about the justice of "I have been overlooked, but now they are overdoing it." Like Herb, I have not been in a situation where I have received praise this week, but I watched the guy who works on our yard. He had a stroke last year and has just become able to do landscaping again.

He came out to trim our yard, and I felt it was important to him to be praised for that. He did a good job. He was like a kid—he was glad to get the money and that was one thing. But to be praised for what a good job he did and for how willing he was, made him light up. It was fun.

I did not have an experience like that for myself this week, but I'll tell you about one from the past. My wife and I went to a charismatic retreat thirty years ago and neither one of us knew what it was. I brought along a bunch of books because I thought it was going to be a quiet three-day weekend.

Wow, was I wrong! It was holy-roller time for all three days! We had a great time. There was this one nun who played the guitar and sang and got everybody going. At first I was like, "Ugh! What are we doing here?" But soon she had us pulled in and had us enjoying it.

Every time we would try to thank her for what she had done, she would say, "Praise God!" I know after a day or two it became frustrating because I wanted to say, "No—thank you for what you are doing—what you as an individual are doing." But I could not get through to her because everything was "Praise God."

It struck me that this was going to be her response regardless of what she did or how much I appreciated it. She deflected all of the praise.

After a couple of days, we caught on that this is how she wanted to handle this. It was her calling to do this and she did not want praise for it.

I have the same reaction that some others have mentioned today. When you get praised, you get embarrassed and instead of praising God it becomes, "Aw shucks," and you don't know what to do. That was always the way when I was a kid.

Now I will remember that if they want to thank me, I can just accept that and let it go. I am not spiritually evolved enough to say "Praise God" and mean it. And I am not to the point where I want to refuse to acknowledge the praise.

I learned from the first two days from trying to thank that nun and trying to get through to her that when someone is on a spiritual plane above where you are, that it takes a while to realize what is going on. At first it feels like a snub when you are trying to thank them and they don't accept it.

For me, I can just say "Thank you" when someone praises me and leave it at that. At my level of development, it would be phony to say "Praise God" unless it was something where a bunch of stuff happened that was clearly beyond my control. Then I might be able to say "Praise God."

LEADER: So I see praise as a good thing, if at the end of the day we can remember that the good comes from God. Maybe you can't say "Praise God!" but at least, in your inner self, you can say, "Okay, I did it, but I know I did not do it on my own."

TRACY: A couple of people mentioned the "Thank you—you're welcome" concept. That takes me back to my own evolution. I was always begging for more praise: "Oh, it was nothing." Then I listened to what I was saying, which was just that I wanted to milk it for a little more!

They were giving me a bit of their heart and true feelings. I was saying it was nothing and I don't accept praise, rather than simply saying "Thank you." Saying "Thank you" acknowledges the thought and the person. It feels much better.

HERB: Sometimes praise is misused. One time, when I came back from Vietnam, I was in San Francisco. I was due for a promotion. The colonel wrote an evaluation. There was nothing on it but praise.

When he gave it to me to sign, I said I felt I was doing a good job but that my performance was overstated. He said if we did not do this I would not get promoted.

I think that praise was used wrongly. I felt I was good enough, but they polished the evaluation up so it looked better. I had not thought about this until we talked about this task. It was praise that was not deserved but the giver had a purpose. I guess I should have just said "Thank you."

LEADER: Thank you, all. You have shown many examples of how each of our tasks generates a wide spectrum of responses. I particularly liked your memories of how you reacted to praise in your past. You remembered what caused some of the beasts to come out of your basement. It is easy to let the beasts come out when you are *high* on praise, isn't it? You will know that you have achieved some success with this task when the love of doing is more powerful than the reward.

Enrichment Reading

1. But when you give alms, do not let your left hand know what your right hand is doing, so that your alms may be done in secret; and your Father who sees in secret will reward you. (Matthew 6:3,4)

2. Angels . . . support their belief that the Lord is the source of every bit of life by observing that everything in the universe goes back to what is good and true. . . . Because angels believe this, they decline any thanks offered them for the good they do. In fact they feel hurt and withdraw if anyone gives them credit for anything good. (Emanuel Swedenborg, *Heaven and Hell* 9)

3. Angels take absolutely no credit to themselves and turn down any praise or admiration for anything they have done, but attribute it all to the Lord. (Emanuel Swedenborg, *Heaven and Hell* 230)

4. If we believed the way things really are, that everything good comes from the Lord and everything evil from hell, then we would not take credit for the good within us or blame for the evil. Whenever we thought or did anything good, we would

focus on the Lord, and any evil that flowed in we would throw back into the hell it came from. But since we do not believe in any inflow from heaven or from hell and therefore believe that everything we think and intend is in us and from us, we make the evil our own and defile the good with our feeling that we deserve it. (Emanuel Swedenborg, *Heaven and Hell* 302)

5. A person ought to do good as though from himself; but when he stops to reflect on the good he is doing or has done, let him think, acknowledge and believe that the Lord, present with him, has accomplished it. (Emanuel Swedenborg, *Secrets of Heaven* 1712)

6. The reward that lasts to eternity is the feeling of joy that comes with loving to do something good with no thought of reward. The Lord pours heaven and eternal happiness into that kind of goodness. (Emanuel Swedenborg, *New Jerusalem* 156)

Task 4

BE USEFUL

 Every day this week, make a conscious effort to put yourself out for the sake of the common good.

- Do at least one thing each day that takes you out of concern for yourself to concern for the welfare of others.
- While doing this task, notice any negative state that comes up for you.

Learning Objectives

- *Recognize that being useful is akin to getting physical exercise—when you are not useful, your spiritual health suffers.*
- *Understand that being useful is the energy that provides for the common good.*
- *See that life is about service and giving, and that being useful is happiness.*
- *Recognize that usefulness is love and charity in action.*

We hear a lot about the work ethic and how, in a sense, we rebel against it. People sometimes say, "I am a human being, not a human doing."

I think that in the past people tended to measure each other too much in terms of what they were doing. If you weren't *doing* something, then you didn't have any worth.

We would like to talk about this idea from the other side, which is that we really are here to serve. That is what life is all about.

With our advanced technology, it is possible for people to go through life being mostly receivers and not givers. Many people have adopted a passive role in life. Part of us is lazy and wants to have things given to us and delivered for our pleasure.

Do you ever feel like you just want to lie down for two or three days? What happens to your body if you lie down for three days? It gets weak! If you want to get really sick, lie down for a month. The body loves to be used.

When we use our minds or bodies to their full extent, we are the most god-like. After all, the center of the universe is life-giving. It is energy that goes out to create and serve. In his writings, Emanuel Swedenborg teaches that the whole of heaven is organized into the form of one human being known as the Universal Human, and also the Body of Christ. Each angel has a function in this Universal Human; so the angels identify themselves according to their use.

Swedenborg says that angels live a useful life. They find their greatest joy in being useful, and that is heavenly happiness. This idea stands in stark contrast to the idea that after you die, your eternal happiness comes from living in a type of retirement home forever. Some people have the idea that there is nothing to do but enjoy ourselves! But how many of us could stand that kind of life? There is something that drives us to a life of service.

Toward the end of his ministry, Jesus did something very dramatic with the disciples. They were at a meal, the Last Supper. At the end of the meal, he got up and washed the disciples' feet. He asked them, "Who is greater, the one who is at the table or the one who serves?"

They answered that it was the person who sits at the table because he can afford to pay the person who serves. Jesus answered, "But I am among you as one who serves" (Luke 22:27).

So the only reason we exist is to make a contribution to the lives of others. We are here to give and not just to get.

The point of this week's task is to have a reminder each day to expend effort to get outside yourself and make a contribution to others. That contribution can take a variety of forms. It can be a simple external thing; it can be a phone call or just listening to someone.

There are so many ways we can make a contribution. We just have to remind ourselves that this is what life is all about. Swedenborg writes that all the senses of the body depend on being used in order to have any fun. Like the sense of touch—it is when you use your hands that you get the fun of touch. Or it is when you use your eyes that you get the fun of seeing. So the joy is in the use, in the function.

I experience some of my greatest love when I have forgotten myself in a task that is totally absorbing. The joy is in being of value to someone else.

TOOLS FOR TASK 4

1. **Notice how being useful makes you feel.** While doing something helpful or useful, take a moment to notice your emotions and thoughts. Where in your "house" do these feelings and thoughts reside?

2. **Notice any energy that comes from serving others.** When helping others with even the most insignificant task, notice

any shift in your own energy. Notice how exercising your useful side is like exercising your physical body. Does your energy increase with both types of exercise?

Participants Report on Task 4

KITTY: Being useful is a blessing and a comfort to me. When I have times of trouble, it opens up a path to circumvent the pain.

It was a good week for this. I spent some time working in the church kitchen, and the task asks if there were any negative feelings. While the kitchen is mostly a wonderful and happy place to be, sometimes people get snappy or overly possessive and I need to stand on my tongue and work through it.

If I can just be a good girl and remember that being Irish is not always a blessing, I can indeed get over it.

But when you have personal things going on inside that are negative, it is a wonderful thing to find usefulness so that you can keep yourself in balance. The balance between the uncomfortable feelings and the feelings of doing a good thing is my area of comfort. It was a wonderful task for me.

JULIE: Being useful this week has definitely worn me out. Lord and angels bless all single caregivers. My most recent use was to tell my neighbor she had lipstick on her teeth. She thanked me profusely.

LEADER: Sometimes the smallest act of kindness can be of great use to those you try to help.

TAMI: I was on a mission trip to Northern Mexico this last weekend. It was a blessing because we have a lot of new people, and when we go to build houses the new people say, "I don't know what to do" or "I don't know if they can use me; I've never done this before." I was able to remind them that if they had not done it before, there would be someone there who could teach them.

I had been given the task of photographing people building the four houses. I was to go from house to house, capturing moments so that others would be able to store these memories. Although I like taking pictures, one challenge came when I was playing with the children and the call came in that the first house was completed.

I HAD THE FALSE IDEA THAT THE "GRAND GOOD" WAS KEY TO THIS TASK.

I did not want to leave, but after snapping a few more photos I hurried over to Team Two. The foreman of this group had been worried because his team consisted of mostly elderly people. He had worried that the house being built by Team Two might get behind the other three because there weren't any young people to help. I felt blessed when I had the opportunity to remind him that we are all children of God and the Lord is orchestrating all that is happening. What a moving event it was that this house was now a home for a wonderful family and it was completed first!

After three more tearful dedications with each family receiving a handmade quilt, curtains, a family Bible, and keys to lock the door, I was anxious to get back to camp for the afternoon. I could not wait to leave and go downtown to find my favorite ice cream store in Rocky Point.

I am constantly amazed at how our dear Father works in our lives. At that very moment I had a dreadful feeling of shame and guilt. I am not sure why, but maybe it had something to do with the selfishness. Driving back to camp and alone with my thoughts, I asked the Lord how I might serve him.

His answer lay in the boxes of peanuts and fruit snacks that were left over from the previous event. I started giving out packages to individuals I saw in the neighborhoods I passed. Some people were washing clothes, some were playing, some were chasing stray dogs from their yard, some were walking, some were tending to children, some were working, some were sitting in the shade, and some were visiting with each other.

But as I greeted them with "*Hola,*" each gifted me with a smile and "*Gracias.*" Many of them even spoke English, saying "Thank you." When my boxes were empty, my spiritual tank was filled with a wonderful feeling of being loved.

I got back to camp and let others know I was leaving to get ice cream if they wanted to come along for a new experience. You have not experienced Mexico until you enjoy the rich, creamy flavor of strawberries. *Fresas con crema* never tasted as good as it did that day. *Gracias,* dear Father—*muchas gracias.*

WHEN MY BOXES WERE EMPTY, MY SPIRITUAL TANK WAS FILLED.

LEADER: So the lesson you learned is that as you become more and more useful, you become more and more happy? Isn't happiness an easy thing to achieve so long as you can do those simple things that help others? Thank you for sharing that.

BOB: I will report on my work. I had the false idea that the "grand good" was key to this task. Only big things were worth contemplating and working on.

A friend of mine sent me an e-mail. He described usefulness in small and trivial things. That friend inspired me to try something new this week. I tried to learn how to be useful in little things.

Each day I found one little task that I would not normally do around the house and did it. One day I made the bed. One day I did sweeping. Another day I hemmed some pants with the sewing machine. One day I noticed someone's windshield needed cleaning so I cleaned it for her. One day I called a friend who had been ailing.

As I progressed through each day, I worked more of these little or middling tasks. I was trying to be useful in different ways each day. But I started to experience some negative thoughts. I caught myself thinking: "No one is noticing what I am doing." As a matter of fact, out of all these things I did, at least one each day, in a whole week only one comment was made: "Oh, I see the maid came in early today!" That generated negativity about this task.

The best spiritual growth aspect of this was that when I did another small task, I said to myself, "I don't care if anyone notices or not. This is making me happy and making me feel good and useful. This is what I think my God wants me to do, even if it is as small as sweeping the floor." So I got to work on little helpful things and forgot about the grandiose good of humanity!

BETSY: I have been thinking about the way things constantly change in our lives. Even our bodies are different than they once were. Over a few years, all the cells have changed. My sense of being useful has also changed.

It may be temporary, but I am now in a place of gratitude for what I have in the moment, because I know things are going to change. Thinking back on the way I used to be useful in a much bigger sense, I am grateful for the opportunity to just serve now.

One way I have served in the last year is taking my granddaughter to gymnastics. Yes, I have other things to do, and yes, it is a big three-hour chunk out of my day. I recognize all the negativity I could get into, but I get so much payoff from those three hours of chattering seven-year-olds, and from watching my granddaughter move for the entire two hours, whether she has to or not. I love listening to her chatter all the way home, too.

Some days, when I am not taking her to class, she wants to show me what she just learned. All that energy and spirit is pure joy, and I get to be a part of that. It is small and simple, but I know God is right in the middle of it. It is something that is changing and will not always be this way. I will not always have this opportunity, so I am blessed that I have it to enjoy right now.

Another thing I noticed about being useful is that for forty-three years we have always had Thanksgiving at our house. But this year we are going to have it at my son's new house and this is different. I am adjusting to that. Part of me is relieved and happy. But I'm seeing how I can be loving and giving in new ways—ways that are different than putting on a big meal.

I find that my state of mind is so much more important than what I am actually doing. If I am making mashed potatoes and am in a grumpy mood while doing it, what is the point? That is not God flowing through me at all. So I decided that in whatever I do, I want to have the right attitude. I want to be a vehicle for God's love in performing a useful deed, or the usefulness loses some of its power.

LEYLA: I was thinking of the ways I was useful this week, and it seems to me that I was the recipient of people's usefulness more than I was useful.

I was talking to a friend who was relating an upset to me. It was funny because the same thing had happened two months ago but she brought it up again and it was the exact same story.

I knew it was going to be a pretty long story, so what I had to do was give up my sense of time and thoughts of what I was planning to do in the next half hour. I tried to just get my ego-mind out of the way and be there in the moment and be a recipient of whatever it was she wanted me to be in her telling of the story. I had to be a patient listener.

I was proud of myself for giving up my ego in that moment, knowing that I was going to be in this conversation for twenty-five minutes. I realized that she just wanted someone to listen and did not expect a response. I tried not to give a response.

For myself, I usually want a listener to nod in agreement with me. I discovered that listening is a gift you can give people. It is multi-faceted and complex. My way of being useful to her was to be quiet except to nod a bit as she was telling the story. In this, not only did I serve her, but I served myself because I gave up my ego and my sense of importance.

I have been thinking a lot about listening. I think it can be very challenging. I have a girlfriend who has a unique gift: when listening, her body language and everything about her is exactly in tune with what you are saying. She always knows the most appropriate thing to say, too.

I started wondering if, when someone is listening to me, do I want them to agree with me? Do I want them to sympathize with me? Do I want them to give me advice or no advice? So listening is quite a challenge.

A Gandhi gem I found: "Speak only if it improves upon the silence."

MICHAEL: I come from a background where use has been a part of my whole life. My mother always preached to be of use to other people; that was the highest goal we could have in life. She forgot to mention that it was important to be useful for yourself as well, but that lesson came along later.

As I worked the task, I was looking for other words for *useful* and I found: *charitable, helpful,* and *worthwhile.* These all seem to be part of the same scheme of things.

On Thursday I was at the grocery store and held the door for someone. They said "Thank you." I thought that was useful. That was it for that day.

Friday, I offered to do a counseling session for someone as a Christmas gift. What was nice about that was that the ego disappeared and it was not a big deal. I woke up that morning singing, "Better watch out, better not cry, Santa Claus is coming to town." I am trying not to think about Christmas because it is way too early, but these things keep popping up. So it was useful to me in that it caused a mood of giving. I think that is my favorite thing about being useful—the giving.

The challenge, of course, is to also accept being on the receiving end.

My brother came in from Seattle on Saturday and we did a lot of useful things, a lot of bonding and talking about family things. We worked together, clearing out the back forty. We watched football and prepared meals together. When he left on Tuesday, I was depressed. I could not think of a way to be useful that day. So I decided that the useful thing for that day was just getting through the day.

Today I gave a class on money and the meaning of life, which was rewarding and useful for the entire class. I enjoy being in that sphere.

VICKY: I did not do anything extraordinary. I did what I normally do—my volunteer work. I feel that doing house things, cooking for someone else, and things like that are useful tasks. But what I worked on was mostly being in the present moment, not doing one thing while having my mind ticking on everything else.

I tried to be on the task I was doing, and seeing the good in doing it the best I could. I tried to enjoy doing it instead of feeling like I had to do it.

LEADER: One lesson I have to remember while working this task is recognizing where I am coming from when I'm trying to do something useful. If I am coming from love, it is satisfying.

If my desire to be useful is coming from charity within me, it means a lot more. I also discovered that many times, when you feel you are being useful to someone else and you don't get recognized, it can make those "resentment" beasts come out of the basement!

Enrichment Reading

1. For who is greater, the one who is at the table, or the one who serves? Is it not the one at the table? But I am among you as one who serves. (Luke 22:27)

2. But when you give alms, do not let your left hand know what your right hand is doing, so that your alms may be done in secret; and your Father who sees in secret will reward you. (Matthew 6:3,4)

3. Doing good things is doing useful things. The amount and quality of usefulness that a given good thing has determines the amount and quality of its goodness. (Emanuel Swedenborg, *True Christianity* 419)

4. Goodwill itself is acting justly and faithfully in our position and our work, because all the things we do in this way are useful to the community; and usefulness is goodness. (Emanuel Swedenborg, *True Christianity* 422)

5. These functionaries are loved, valued, and respected to the extent that they do not attribute their use to themselves but to the Lord. To that extent they are wise, and to that extent they fulfill their uses from good motives. (Emanuel Swedenborg, *Heaven and Hell* 390)

Task 5

LET GO OF RUSHING

 Observe yourself rushing, and experiment with letting go of the need to rush.

- Notice the physical and emotional symptoms you have when you are rushing. Observe the thoughts that justify your condition of haste, and test to see if those thoughts are correct.

- Notice what you were doing before feeling rushed, and what you do afterward.

- Experiment with letting go of these feelings, separating your higher self from your irrational, emotional self. Use the affirmation: "It is rushing, but I don't have to."

Learning Objectives

- *Understand that rushing causes you to miss the important aspects of what you are doing.*

- *See that rushing is the enemy of serenity and peace.*

- *Understand that rushing diverts attention and makes waste.*

Part of the theme of spiritual growth is that all things we face in our lives can be affected by negative emotions. It is almost as if these emotions are opportunistic diseases. You know the saying, "Haste makes waste."

I find that I do some of my best rushing when I am sitting still. An example is going to the airport to catch a plane. I might be driving the car, waiting at a stoplight, and I am rushing. I am standing in line, waiting to get my ticket, and I am rushing, standing perfectly still! Then I am sitting on the plane and I am rushing while waiting for takeoff. All this rushing is obviously an "inside job." This rushed feeling is destroying my peace and the pleasure of my trip. We need to fight off those rushing beasts and resist their infection.

The rushing infection includes negative feelings that have a certain flavor to them. I have learned to identify those feelings and to recognize the negative thoughts. The negative thoughts act to confuse the mind; they make it harder for me to see and think and act.

And then there is tripping over things and dropping things when you rush. There is a touching story in the Bible of King Saul's son, who was literally crippled by rushing. When his nurse heard about the battle in which King Saul was killed, she rushed and dropped the child, and he became lame in both feet. He referred to himself as a "dead dog" because of being lame.

To slow down and go with the pace of whatever is happening is very hard. This task is a variation on living in the present. You can just go with real time—don't you love that expression, "real time"? Rushing is not real time; it is very messy time. So what I would like you to do this week, whenever you find yourself rushing, is to become an observer and look at the different aspects of your rushing: the feelings, the thoughts, and the actions.

Then use the affirmation, "It is rushing, but I don't have to," and see if you can rise above the rushing state.

I find this task very challenging. Just a few minutes ago, I was rushing and it seemed silly since I was just about to speak on the subject.

Rushing is an enemy of things like serenity and peace. What we do is allow the negative to deprive us of something we prize. Often we will blame it on the circumstances: "Of course I am rushing, because . . ." Well, if you believe that, you will believe anything. You are rushing because the negative beast (the rushing beast) has you by the leg and he is opportunistic.

I could be rushing right now, couldn't I? Maybe some of you are rushing right now. But if I make up reasons for why I am rushing and why I have to rush, then it is almost impossible to let go of the beast because you have to wait for the circumstance to change.

Often the circumstance does not have any time schedule to it. It is like driving to the airport; it is already pretty well determined when the car will get there. The rushing has no effect on the outcome. Or, if you are driving the car, rushing has a dangerous effect.

The Bible says, "In quietness and in trust shall be your strength" (Isaiah 30:15). That is part of letting go.

TOOLS FOR TASK 5

1. **Remember a time when you were rushing.** Did the rushing result in a payoff, or did it incur a penalty? What emotions did you experience while you were rushing? Were they constructive or destructive?

2. **Observe yourself when you feel the need to rush.** Do you feel rushing will help with the task you are undertaking? Do you feel compelled to react to the demands of others? Can you

sense that rushing is the enemy of serenity and peace of mind? Stop to notice whether the rushing and its companion, stress, are contributing to what you wish to accomplish.

Participants Report on Task 5

TRACY: I was in Connecticut where I had worked previously. This was a focused week where I had to do a good job. It was one of those schedules where I just had to work all day, then go back to the hotel and get ready for the next day.

The task came to me by e-mail after you had all met that night, and I tucked it away because I was so busy. I needed to leave the hotel by 5:45 a.m. to allow myself enough time to get to the airport, and I left at 6:15. I was not sure where the airport rental car spot was. I was getting tense while driving down the highway. That was the first moment that the task came to mind, because I remembered I was not supposed to rush.

The second time rushing happened, I followed the rental agency's directions to their location but still could not find them. I started to wonder what would happen if I did not get there in time. So I stopped, found the phone number, and asked them how to get there. They gave me directions and I found it, but the airport shuttle had just left! One thing after another tested me as I tried to work this "not rushing" task.

YOU WILL STILL GET THERE AND WILL BE IN A MORE PEACEFUL STATE OF MIND IF YOU DO NOT RUSH.

They reassured me that the shuttle driver was quick and would return in ten minutes. I worried that this would not be fast enough, but I had other things to do, like get my bags out. It was pouring rain. I knew it was possible that I could still get to the airport but not be able to check my bags, and that would not be a good thing. The van returned in about five minutes and I got to the airport. I was certain from the beginning that by letting go of rushing nothing would change except that I would get where I was going in a more peaceful way. That has been what I have experienced all week.

I find myself doing this task enthusiastically, because I do rush from one thing to another and another. I wear several hats during the day, and as I speed from one thing to another I sometimes find myself saying, "You will still get there and will be in a more peaceful state of mind if you do not rush." Letting go of rushing has been wonderful. I love this task. I have learned that not much bad happens if I just stay back and slow down.

LEADER: Most of the rushing occurs inside our brains. The rushing beast likes to take control of the moment, telling you that all sorts of bad things will happen because you are "late, late, late and far too important to waste time!"

TRACY: Totally! My car's speedometer was at 65 or 70, but the beast in my head was yelling, "Go faster! Go faster!" It was the letting go and backing up and clearing of my mind that helped. I felt more in touch with my spirit.

JULIE: I also had a lot of fun with this task because I also zip from one thing to the other.

A lot of times I don't even finish what I was doing previously. So I started out by just concentrating on finishing one small task at a time, which was a real challenge but also very freeing. I learned that I can do this. I don't have to spin in circles all the time. I tried to stop kicking myself for not finishing things. This was freeing, and it helped me concentrate.

It was an appropriate time to do this task, at the beginning of the holiday season. I was grateful for that. Several times on the check-out line in different stores, when I noticed someone behind me with only one or two items, I let them in front of me because I was not in a hurry. They were very appreciative of that.

The latest experience was this afternoon. I had to get my niece to an appointment, and we were scheduled to arrive with just enough time after picking her up somewhere else. We drove near my house, but I needed to veer off to go straight to the appointment. My niece said, "We're going home first, right?" And I said, "No, we don't have time for that. We are going straight to the appointment." She said she had to use the bathroom. So my mind snapped with anger and frustration. The "not rushing" balloon popped and I could already picture us entering the office late. So I decided that I was overreacting and that, since she needed to use the bathroom, we could make a simple detour. So we went home.

As we got back on route, I said a little prayer to the angels in my head, that I wanted all green lights and that I would not speed. If I was late, I would be late and that would be okay. I was looking at the clock and we were now ten minutes behind schedule. I was cruising along, not speeding, and sure enough passed a sheriff on his motorcycle with his radar gun and thought, "Oh, I am doing so well! I love this task!" We arrived at the office at the minute we were supposed to be there. I can thank the angels for stretching out time. I learned to slow down and focus. The task was very helpful.

BETSY: I was amazed that in two weeks I did not feel myself physically rushing. But mentally I noticed five or six times where I was telling myself that I had so much to do that I would not be able to do it all. My pattern is to lament that I have so much to do and have no help.

This puts me right in the basement. It totally robs me of the present moment. It robs me of any kind of Christmas spirit. It makes me agitated and scattered. I skip from one thing to another. I will work on one thing for a little bit and then skip to something else, so I feel like I am in a whirlwind. Even though I am not physically rushing, my brain will not slow down.

I did a couple things that helped. I made a list and tried to adjust my attitude. I have a new book that I designated as my "holiday book." Anything I needed to remember or wanted to work on, I wrote down. That helped me, to get it down on paper and out of my head. I am afraid I am going to forget things, so if I write it down, I can let it go.

Then I worked on my attitude and thought, "If I can't do this thing with love, then I am not doing it." That helped more than anything. It reminded me of the main point.

The most significant thing I realized is that no matter how much I am doing or how rushed I am, there is nothing right now more important than my spiritual growth. So why would I let ten minutes get in the way of that? Or why would I let someone else get in the way of that?

Those adjustments really helped me slow down. It could not be better timing for this task. God certainly has a sense of humor.

KITTY: I'd like to borrow the word "scattered" because it seems to creep up. In practicing patience, which I think is part and parcel of this project, I discovered that when I rush I have to do things two or three times.

I rush off to the bank only to find the shopping list is still at home. So back I go, because I had focused on only one thing and rushed.

For me, to avoid rushing is the discipline of patience. I have gone back to making lists that no one else can understand because they have arrows and circles, but they mean things to me. With my lists, I am not going down the same street in the same direction two or three times a day just because I did not take a moment to slow down. As you said, this is the season for this task. It is a good lesson.

LEYLA: It seems like even when I was in college I developed the habit of rushing. I would go back to my dorm to eat lunch. You had only so much time to eat before the next class, so you just rushed through the line needing to eat.

For me, it is very habit-forming. Some of my worst habits are entrenched in rushing. I might have plenty of time but am still in rushing mode. I have analyzed that a lot. I have even said that I was going to get up an hour earlier and stay up an hour later just to give myself more time, and that does help a little bit.

I am a pretty good planner and usually plan my time well. Where I have a real challenge is when the rushing is incorporated with driving on the road. When you are rushing to point A, then B, then C, you might have forgotten something, and you might have to drive out of your way.

For example, this week I left my billfold sitting in the grocery cart in the parking lot after I had put the groceries in my car. So I was unloading groceries at home and realized my billfold was missing. I had to get back in the car and wasn't rushing a bit. I knew what the traffic was going to be like and I was determined not to rush.

I had lost my billfold before and I was going to take precautions this time. I told myself to calm down and that it was probably still in the middle of the parking lot. Maybe someone took it or maybe someone turned it in. I thought over what was in the billfold: my driver's license, a debit card, and a credit card. Those three things would be an inconvenience to lose, but I knew I could handle that. When this happened to me about six months ago, I wasn't sure what was in the billfold!

I drove reasonably well and thought over what I would have to do if the billfold was completely gone. I would have to get my driver's license again and all that. I got back to the parking lot and went into the store and went to the customer service person. He was helping someone do a wire transfer and the customer did not speak English, so it was going to be a long process! I said, "Excuse me, but has anyone turned in a billfold?" Someone had, and I feel very fortunate that I got it back.

I find myself in traffic a lot and need to calm myself. I think that when I am at the height of rushing, my body is in a state of tension and I am spiritually asleep. That is the ultimate form of us not being spiritually awake, when we are rushing, because we are operating on a mechanical level, not a spiritual level.

HERB: I have not had any rushing experience for some time. In fact, this afternoon I was saying to my wife that I have nothing to report and asked her if she could give me an idea for what I might talk about. She said, "I don't think you've rushed since you got shot at." I'm going to have to pass since it has been a long time since I rushed.

BOB: On Thanksgiving Day we made plans to eat with friends. It was a beautiful day outside and I said to myself, "I can accomplish some outside things before we go to dinner." I learned something about the rushing beast that lives within me by this experience.

I went out to clean the car and do a few things in the yard. I discovered that for everything I needed to do, there were two more things that needed to be done.

Have you had that experience where the tasks in front of you just seem to multiply? All of the sudden I just said, "I can't get all of this done before I have to get cleaned up for dinner with our friends." Then I woke up and said, "You are not going to rush through this. It is a holiday and you are looking forward to going to dinner with these people. Let's pay attention to who just made this schedule up that caused the rushing."

What I learned was that I am the primary schedule maker for the rushing beast. It is me who puts the pressure on me to do too many things within a given amount of time. And I said, "You know what? That has been true my whole life." I have forced myself to try to do too many things with the resources that I have had. There is something inside me that's driven to make me do it.

I learned something about myself from this exercise. I wrote in my journal: (1) It is *my* schedule; (2) I made the schedule; (3) I can violate the schedule.

So that is how I worked the "not rushing" task. I learned that *I* am the "rushing beast" in my life!

MICHAEL: My last two weeks have not been going fast. I thought this task would be a piece of cake.

Then I discovered that there is good rushing and bad rushing. The good rushing is like when we were on Air Force alert, we had five minutes to get airborne when the bell went off. So the bell would ring and you rush out to the airplane. But in good rushing you have prepared everything ahead so the parachute is in the seat, someone is there to start the engine, and off you go.

Bad rushing is when I am not thinking and suddenly have to go find everything I need. Then I am always behind and am distracted.

I got tested while driving. I don't know why driving challenges us all! Driving down here tonight, there was some idiot weaving in and out and I had to work hard on the task. You don't get a lot of time when this comes up. He swerved; I went over and could not help myself. I flashed my bright lights at him just to let him know what a problem he was. I knew what I was doing and got back in the flow of things.

It is a great task. I can look calm on the outside, but I am much more aware as a result of this task that when the bad rushing gets in my head I need to reorient.

JACK: I agree, this task is timely. A couple times I caught myself rushing and reminded myself of the task. I don't need to rush.

Last night someone wanted to meet me near where I live. They asked me to be there in half an hour. I wanted to cooperate but thought there was no chance I could get there on time. I needed to take some sort of preventive action, so I told them it was not realistic in rush hour traffic and that it would be more like forty-five minutes. They said that was okay as long as it was not more than that.

WHEN I AM AT THE HEIGHT OF RUSHING . . . I AM SPIRITUALLY ASLEEP.

I told them I could not guarantee I could make it, but assured them that I had their phone number and would call if it was getting too late. It is unlike me to do that; normally I am a people-pleaser and if you say, "Can you meet me at the top of Mount Lemmon in fifteen minutes?" I would agree. Obviously they were not very pleased about adjusting the time, but I was in this flow of traffic, and when I did miss three or four traffic lights at the same intersection I was glad to get there in just under the forty-five minutes.

Then on the way back, with no time limit, two clowns decided to wreck in front of me! I took this personally. It wasn't much of a wreck, but there was nowhere to get off the road. Then cops came, and more cops came. They eventually eased the cars off the road, which in my experience they almost never do. They usually take pictures and put up cones and so on.

One thing that dawned on me was that my reaction was very unkind. These people did not wreck their cars to interfere with Jack's day. I think they caused themselves far more problems than they caused me, but I had been very unsympathetic—until the cops and ambulances arrived. After a while it became funny, because I was thinking how cruel and uncaring I was being. It was all because I was thinking I needed to hurry. Clearly I have no control over these matters and need to chill out.

The task has been a good reminder that there is a certain amount of humility that goes with not rushing. How much control do I have over a situation? If I am going to be late, would I be better off admitting it in advance and rescheduling it?

BETSY: Recently, I have really worked at not rushing. I do pretty well most of the time. I make lists.

I read this task every morning to keep it in my mind. When I found myself getting a little anxious and rushed, I would just tell myself everything was going to work out. I am not rushing around anymore like I used to. It took a lot of work, but I like it this way. It works for me.

LEADER: I think it works for all of us. When that rushing beast stays in the basement, we can work on our spiritual well-being.

TAMI: I call it "Hurry up and wait," because that is often what life is all about for me. I rush to get to work, only to wait to clock in. I rush to answer the phone and wait on someone who puts me on hold. I rush to the next traffic signal to wait until the light turns green. I rush to get ready for a party and wait until the guests arrive. I rush to get home from work and wait to watch a TV program. I rush to the bank before it closes to wait in line for a teller. I rush to the grocery store and wait in line to check out.

This week, I made a conscious effort not to rush.

I was driving down the road and saw a "required check engine" light on my dashboard. Now, I have seen "check engine," but this said "*required*" and it was in red!

I was really hungry and thought I would hurry over to the dealership with my car, but I had not had lunch and it was four o'clock. I was not going to rush! I didn't even use the drive-through! I went into the restaurant and got my lunch.

I phoned the dealership, but it was after four o'clock. They would not receive cars after four thirty and they knew I could not get there in time. I said I was driving out to Oklahoma and that I would get the truck serviced when I got back. This was a three-thousand-mile round trip but I didn't care since I was not rushing, even if it was required! So he said he would call me back.

THERE IS A CERTAIN AMOUNT OF HUMILITY THAT GOES WITH NOT RUSHING.

I put my lunch in a to-go pack and drove over to the dealership just in case (since he was not going to rush and call me back after four thirty anyway). I was parked at the dealership and my phone rang. He said, "We can service your truck." I pulled over and he said, "Where were you?" I explained and he asked if I had rushed over. I said, "Funny that you mentioned the word *rushed* because I didn't. It is my spiritual growth task."

I explained to him about the task, and he thought the whole thing was funny. It was refreshing, because you have to go over in your mind that if they can help you they can, and if they can't, you can't worry about it. I finished my lunch while I waited for my truck to be serviced and did not feel rushed. Everything fell into place.

My experience with this task reminded me of a joke I heard that started out, "Dear Mom and Dad, I am writing this letter real slow so you can read it!"

My friend said he uses this prayer a lot: "God grant me patience, and grant it to me right now."

LEADER: I find myself doing "internal" rushing in traffic also. I feel somehow that I am responsible for policing all these drivers. You know how you get that feeling? You flash your lights one time, like Michael described earlier. My wife often pokes me and tells me to stop. I say, "Well, someone has to tell them how rude they are!"

From all your reports, it is clear that the rushing beast can take control any time we let it.

I believe that the beast really likes to feed on our ego: "I'm too important to be wasting my time!" It also likes to feed on our fears: "What will happen if I'm late to that important appointment?"

In my life, the beast makes me lose sight of what is important in the present moment. I am conditioned to place too much importance on time management. After all, I am an "executive"! But I miss far too much by worrying about time. I can't wait for the peace that comes with the lack of time consciousness that Swedenborg describes as the mind-set of the angels.

Enrichment Reading

1. I waited patiently for the Lord; he inclined to me and heard my cry. (Psalms 40:1)

2. When we are being reborn—which is accomplished by having spiritual truth and goodness planted in us and having falsity and evil moved aside—we are reborn slowly, not quickly. (Emanuel Swedenborg, *Secrets of Heaven* 9334:2)

3. The more haste, ever the worst speed. (Winston Churchill)

4. They stumble that run fast. (William Shakespeare)

5. When we are in a state of heavenly love or emotion, we are in an angelic state. We seem to step outside of time if there is no impatience in our mood.... The emotions involved in real love draw us out of our bodily and worldly concerns, lifting our mind toward heaven and freeing us from the restraints of time. (Emanuel Swedenborg, *Secrets of Heaven* 3827)

Task 6

STOP GIVING ADVICE

 Spend the next twenty-four hours observing your impulse to give advice, directly or indirectly. After that first day of self-observation, stop giving advice for a whole week.

- Keep in mind that you are doing this task for the sake of your own spiritual growth, and not to deprive other people of your wisdom.
- If for some reason you feel you must give advice, do so only from a higher place in yourself.

Learning Objectives

- *Notice that others will survive without your input or direction.*
- *Recognize that advice-giving takes you out of the spiritual growth mode of seeking guidance from your Higher Power.*
- *Understand that advice-giving shows a lack of respect and can hurt interpersonal relationships.*
- *Understand that advice-giving can be detrimental in that it devalues the other person's ability to exercise his or her own insight and will.*

There is something inside us that loves to help. But when the ego gets involved, this desire to help is almost a disease.

Giving advice comes from a suspect part of us. When we are in the advice-giving mode, we get out of the spiritual growth mode. Maybe it is just that we would like a little relief from our problems. We don't have to think about our own problems if we think about someone else's problems.

Maybe you have had the experience of someone telling you what to do. I find that annoying. For one thing, it puts me down! They are the expert, I am the fool. I am subject to the bounty of their great wisdom.

A friend of mine used to say advice is the easiest thing in the world to give as long as you don't have to live with the consequences. Have you ever given or received advice that turned out to be really disastrous?

Once, when someone asked me for advice and I was foolish enough to give it, I offered my wonderful suggestion and this person said, "I already tried that." I asked how it worked out and they said, "It was terrible, the worst thing I ever did!" So I had just told this person to do something that (a) they had already tried, and (b) had already proven to be a mistake.

As the advice receiver, I think of when I was driving from city to city in England, before they had superhighways. I got frustrated with the twisty, turning roads. One time I wanted to pass the car I was following but could never see far enough ahead to pass. Finally the driver ahead signaled me to pass. Despite my frustration, something told me not to follow that advice. Seconds later an oncoming car sped by! I would have been dead!

The Bible has some wonderful stories about advice-giving. When the prosperous King Solomon died, his son Rehoboam inherited an unstable kingdom. People from the northern tribes came and said,

"We have been laboring under these terrible taxes and difficult conditions. Can you ease up a little bit?" So he went and asked his counsel for advice. He was told they were right and he should ease up.

He disliked that advice so he consulted another advisor, who told him, "Oh these people, if you give them an inch they will take a mile. Be tough on them." So he was tough on them and they rebelled. The country split in half and never got back together again, all because of bad advice.

Like Solomon's son, we tend to select the advice we want to follow. We rarely give up the power of decision to someone else.

There are several fundamental problems with the advice game. First, when someone opens up to you and you shift into advice-giving mode, at that point you have stopped listening. In your mind, you have already solved their problem and are just waiting for a space in the conversation where you can give your advice.

The second problem is that advice-giving shows a lack of respect for the other person. It is telling them that they do not know how to run their life but you do.

The third problem is that people in the habit of seeking and taking advice get into an unhealthy spiritual state, because they are not using their own freedom and reason.

One of the things I loved about my upbringing was that there were so many kids in our family that Mom and Pa hardly ever told us what to do. They hardly ever knew what we were doing. The message I got was, "You are smart. Figure it out."

So we each use our own brain and best judgment. The assumption of Task 6 is that people will be able to survive without you giving them advice for a week.

TOOLS FOR TASK 6

1. **Explore the two sides of advice: giving and receiving.**
   Recall a time when you gave advice to someone else. How did

the receiver of your advice react? Look to see where that advice came from in your mind. Did your advice come from that loving part of yourself that wanted to be helpful, or was it driven by your ego to prove your own importance, knowledge, or control? Now reflect on times when you were given advice. How did you feel as the receiver? Was the advice coming from the love and charity of the giver?

2. **Recall the results of your advice.** Was your advice helpful? Was it followed? Did it affect your relationship with that person? Did it help or hinder their personal development?

3. **Did you consult your Higher Power before giving advice?** We have something inside us that loves to help. Perhaps the love to help comes from our Higher Power. Or perhaps it comes from a need to prove our superiority or sense of worth. Consider the source of your own advice before offering it. Are there other methods of helping—such as being a good listener?

Participants Report on Task 6

KITTY: I tried to stop giving advice as the task suggests. Then my son asked, "Why are you so remote?" This made me aware that I had been giving advice forever. Without advice, my communication with him became a void. I wasn't giving him the advice that he came to me expecting I would give!

So it is a complicated dance. If you have kids, you might feel it is part of your parental duty to share the great wonder of your years of experience and wisdom. So I learned that if someone says, "What do you think?" that is not permission to give them advice.

BETSY: My son and I discuss a lot of things in our lives. He is really hungry to find out how I think about things. I told him the task was "Stop giving advice" and that I want to be careful not to give advice.

He said, "I never think of you as giving me advice. You never tell me what to do. I just want to know what you think."

I mulled the idea that if I told him what I thought and he agreed and then went through with that action as a result, he might not think it was his own decision. He did not agree at all. He likes to gather information and hear what other people think. Then he makes his own decision.

COMPASSIONATE LISTENING IS COMING FROM A HIGHER PLACE.

I realized it's important for me to be a good listener and pick up on when my turn for talking is finished and when I need to tune in to how he is processing what I said. It is a totally different thing. Compassionate listening is coming from a higher place. It's not that you think you are superior or that you know it all. It's not that you think you know what is best for somebody.

It's a slippery slope. He came by and put up my Christmas lights. He did it his way! That is exactly how he said it: "I put up the Christmas lights," and then, pause, "My way." They were different. I right away practiced not saying anything but had to laugh.

JACK: I had an awakening to a line that I heard many times on television. You've heard of Dr. Phil? He's always saying, "So how's that working out for you?"

It just occurred to me this week what that means. It can mean a lot of criticism: "Boy is that stupid." So you decided that you would go up on a ladder in the mud knowing that some of the rungs on the ladder were broken and it was tilting. So you fell and broke your arm—so, how's that working out for you? If you just point out how people are making poor decisions, it brings them up short because it is a form of advice-giving.

I did have the opportunity to quell one round of criticism. One of my relatives was criticizing another relative, and my urge was to criticize the one relative for criticizing the other one. I wanted to say, "Stop doing that!" But that would have put me in the same position as relative one in what he was doing to relative two.

So I thought it better to refrain from criticism. I concluded that it would not have been appropriate to say, "How is that working for you?" because it would not be helpful.

TRACY: Because of the kinds of training and coaching I do, I have been mentored by someone who has taught me a personal maxim: "I don't give advice." The coaching style is to ask questions like, "Would you like to set a goal to do that?" or "What obstacles do you see?" So I have this mental caveat, "Oh, I am a perfect person, I never give advice!"

When the need to give advice flames up and is about to percolate into action, I would always think it was okay to give business-related advice. The one place I've been conscious of not giving business advice has been with my fiancée, who I think could be doing many things differently in his business. This weekend I made a point of not saying anything, but I realized how much advice I *had* given to him about something I know nothing about.

In my own business, I felt miserable about giving advice to my partner. I told her, "My spiritual growth task for the week is not giving advice." She said, "But this is business, it's not the same." So she was saying I could put my two cents in when I am involved. When I'm not, then I've been careful not to give advice.

My last example: My son is taking care of my house in Ohio. He called to alert me that a large accident had occurred with diseased trees overhanging the house, and it involved a lot of money in roof damage. It was dark, rainy, and cold. He said he was looking in the attic with a flashlight. I found myself saying, "It might be better to take care of it tomorrow."

So it was a motherly thing. I was not aware until we went through this task how many times I do that with people. I mother people a lot. It just comes out so naturally unless I'm thinking about the task. So I discovered there isn't anybody that I don't mother!

I INSTINCTIVELY WANT TO GIVE ADVICE . . .
EVEN IF I DON'T KNOW WHAT THEY SHOULD DO.

JULIE: This was a hard task for me. I decided to just hide from everybody. Before I would answer someone's question, I'd consider all the gray areas: Is it guidance? Is it feedback? Is it my opinion? Is it a recommendation? I have this way of justifying my recommendations, like what books to read, what movies to see, and which ones not to see. If someone asked my advice and wouldn't take it, I would probably be offended.

I kept hearing the voice of my sixth-grade teacher. He would pound his fist on the desk and say, "Am I right or am I right?" It was that whole gesture, how he would move his fist—everything came back to me: "Am I right or am I right?"

When I did find myself in a situation where someone asked for advice, or if I wanted advice, what I could focus on was: "What do they want?" or "What do I want?"

I also thought of Dr. Phil saying, "How is that working for you?" I find it a little sarcastic, but I also find it impressive. I thought if I could change that a little bit, to "Well, what do you want or need?" when someone is asking my advice, that it would make it easier for them to seek their own solution.

If I could identify what I needed or wanted, then I would not need to seek outside advice. However, I found myself at the doctor's office and, instead of asking him what to do, I was telling him what I needed. It was actually quite refreshing to say what I was feeling and experiencing. I could do what was recommended but also state what I needed. He made a shift in the treatment plan and I felt really good all week.

This has been a refreshing task, but I did want to run from it.

BOB: I had an interesting experience, becoming aware of advice-giving in a whole new way. I made myself aware of advice-giving while driving. I discovered that flashing the lights, yelling, and gesturing while driving was a way of giving advice to fellow drivers on the road.

We were told for the first twenty-four hours to observe what we were doing. On the day after our meeting, I was slowed down on a one-lane road by somebody doing 25 mph in a 40 mph zone. I proceeded to give advice by flashing my lights at them in their rearview mirror. When I got down to the University of Arizona area, people were jaywalking, and I was shaking my finger, advising them that this was dangerous.

I observed myself doing this. I know no one gave a darn about the advice I was giving them, but it was a form of advice-giving, wasn't it? I realized that to do this task, I would have to go the rest of the week without flashing, honking, and gesturing! For me, that was going to be very hard.

I made it all the way to Friday, but that morning I had an eight o'clock appointment with my eye doctor and he was going to run some special tests. I was nervous and concerned. I started driving down a major thoroughfare to get across town. What happened? I got three or four blocks down the main street, and a construction truck pulled out in front of me in a one-lane construction zone. It was obviously a supervisor; he was doing 5 mph in a 45 mph zone, watching and organizing his crew. He was talking on the phone!

I told myself: "You are not supposed to flash him; you are not supposed to give him that kind of advice. You certainly aren't going to honk at him, are you?" Wrong. When he turned off the road I managed to gesture, as a show of respect for him. So what can I say? The important part of this task is that I became aware of a very negative thing in my life: letting other people upset me and reacting with useless gestures! I did not need to advise them that they are rude and insensitive to my needs.

I made it to the doctor's appointment on time, and the tests came out okay. Everything worked out fine except that I felt pretty bad about the way I had reacted. At least I was aware that this is a form of advice-giving that I had not noticed before. I am going to try to do better.

TAMI: I instinctively want to give advice. When someone says something to me, I immediately want to respond with advice and let them know what to do, even if I really don't know what they should do. I had never given it much thought.

My conclusion was that I needed to lock myself in the closet for the week and have no contact with others. I would still have myself to deal with. I am actually worse about giving myself advice.

People know I like to talk, but I tried to become more aware of the advice-giving part of my conversations.

I work as a volunteer at an information booth. The job is not to give advice; it is to give information. I recognize that in an information setting you can give someone information without giving advice. The hard part was that I still wanted to give advice. For example, you can give someone an address, but I would take them outside to point where they should go and how they should get there!

There was another incident where I mentioned to a new friend that I had dabbled in investments. A couple of days later he said he wanted advice, and that it was about investments. I instinctively thought, "I don't give advice, especially when it comes to investments." So I found myself engaged in this conversation advising him not to take advice.

Throughout this week, I would let people know I couldn't give advice. But one piece of advice that I always give is to go with your heart. I tend to think that what I feel in my heart is from God, that higher spiritual soul.

I had a phone call from my son (I always tell him my spiritual growth tasks), and he asked how I am doing. He said his friend Mike was visiting, and asked if I wanted to talk to him. I said, "Sure."

He said, "Wait, Mike does not want to talk to you because he doesn't want to be lectured." I immediately thought, "I see I am giving him a lot of advice, for him to not want to talk to me." I have known this kid for years. I said, "You tell Mike to get on the phone. My spiritual growth task is to not give advice, so I can't lecture him."

I learned that my advice-giving was lecturing. The good part was that we joked about it and I told him I could not give advice this week. We had a nice conversation. It goes back to Tracy talking about the mothering. I just naturally do that.

I noticed that I consciously led the conversation in a different direction. I had a nice conversation and found myself listening more than trying to tell others what to do. I learned a lot more about the other person by refraining from giving advice.

This was a tough assignment. It was not an easy thing for me, and it is still in my mind.

LEADER: I may be wrong, but I am hearing that somehow "mothering" or "fathering" with advice-giving is good, and "lecturing" with advice-giving is bad. Is that what I am hearing?

"Mothering" or "fathering" is an *excuse* for advice-giving! Perhaps it is a way of saying that the advice is coming from a higher place inside you. That is a good thing to remember about advice-giving.

VICKY: Not giving advice was very challenging. I am aware when I am around friends that I don't give advice unless I am asked. But I didn't realize how much I do give advice until I was given this task.

The first two days were very hard because I was constantly giving unsolicited advice. It got better as the week went on, because I was more aware of it. I would catch myself as I would start to say something. In my mind I was still doing it, but I thought I was getting really good because I wasn't verbally giving advice. However, I was still thinking in my mind that they should do it this way or that way.

My week was interesting and challenging, but I am more aware of how often I jump forward to give advice now because I never had to think about it before.

IF YOU ARE GOING TO GIVE ADVICE, BE AWARE OF WHERE THAT ADVICE IS COMING FROM.

LEYLA: I am going to continue to work this task because this topic is fascinating to me.

It seems to me that when you live with someone, there is a lot of advice-giving about things and processes. It could be about something as mundane as putting the cap on the toothpaste. Well, I don't live with anyone so I don't really have that issue at home. My family is where I had the negative experiences in giving advice.

I don't like to give advice because I like to leave people in freedom. I don't like hearing advice myself because it's denigrating, especially as I am getting older. I want to say, "How do you think I got here?"

Last weekend, I went to a major church function. It was absolutely wonderful. I was talking to someone the next day about a couple of things that had happened, and coming out of my mouth was: "Next year, hopefully they will do something different." So you see that was advice in a way. It was not given to the person directly; it was indirect, in the form of gossiping.

I noticed when Bob told us about the signals he gave on the road that advice can be nonverbal. What about body language? I often use the raised eyebrow! I would rather give advice that way. It is so incorporated in our lives.

I was talking with a friend. I told her about my brother and some health issues he was having. I am upset about this. She said, "You better get yourself tested" (because we are siblings).

I was observing the advice being given to me. I was trying to be chill and keep a neutral expression on my face, and she went on about how I needed to get tested. She asked if I agreed, because I was not responding. I was stewing and defending myself in my head.

LEADER: An important aspect of spiritual growth is to learn how to keep from reacting mechanically. It sounds like all of us were on the same track. We hadn't realized how often we are tempted to give advice without thinking. Even if we learn only that, we can run our potential advice through our brain and get away from giving it automatically. We might be able to get away from our mechanical reactions when giving or receiving advice.

One thing common to all groups that reported on this task is that, whether you call it mothering or fathering or just good advice-giving, you are never going to break the habit of giving advice. It is always going to happen in one form or another, whether it's silent body language or a downright "You shouldn't do that!" or "You should do this!"

The main point that comes out loud and clear is that, if you are going to give advice, be aware of where that advice is coming from. Is it coming from the ego that says I know better than you do, or is it from that "mothering" or "fathering" instinct that says I love this person and I want them to make the right choices and to do the right thing? You can make this distinction only when you are aware that you are giving advice.

It was also interesting to hear what many of you said about the internal dialog. When we worked the task on not rushing, we all came up with the internal hurry and the external hurry. Now with this task, we are doing the same thing. We recognize how strong the "advice beast" is even if we hold it inside ourselves. I wonder if more of the tasks have an internal and external quality to them.

Enrichment Reading

1. It is a good divine that follows his own instructions. I can easier teach twenty what were good to be done than be one of the twenty to follow mine own teaching. (William Shakespeare)

2. Nothing is less sincere than our mode of asking and giving advice. He who asks seems to have a deference for the opinion of his friend, while he only aims to get approval of his own and make his friend responsible for his action. And he who gives advice repays the confidence supposed to be placed in him by a seemingly disinterested zeal, while he seldom means anything by his advice but his own interest or reputation. (François de La Rochefoucauld)

3. Advice is seldom welcome. Those who need it most, like it least. (Samuel Johnson)

4. Giving advice is sometimes only showing our wisdom at the expense of another. (Anthony Shaftesbury)

5. Oh, rebellious children, says the Lord, who carry out a plan, but not mine; who make an alliance, but against my will, adding sin to sin." (Isaiah 30:1)

6. The ones who have the Lord's permission to talk with us never say anything that would take away our freedom to think rationally; and they do not teach, either. Only the Lord teaches us. (Emanuel Swedenborg, *Divine Providence* 135)

Task 7

OVERCOME THE WORLD

 When you are upset by some event, situation, or person, and you wish things would change, turn your attention inward and upward.

- Change the context of your experience so that you find its positive value.

- Transform the situation.

Learning Objectives

- *Recognize that you can alter a difficult situation by working on yourself.*

- *See that you can base your life experience on input from your Higher Power, and not on input from evil.*

- *Understand that when you are cut off from your Higher Power, you are absent the influence that enables you to face the world with peace and serenity.*

- *Understand that evils and falsities can proliferate in your awareness, destroying the quality of your life, unless you actively prevent them from taking control.*

So many things concern us in our daily lives. We worry about our finances, health, security, and relationships. And there is so much in life that angers us: crime, corruption, and many forms of abuse. Often we feel helpless. It seems as if the world is a mess and there is not much that one individual can do.

When Jesus said, "Be of good cheer, I have overcome the world" (John 16:33), what did that mean? Did it mean something significant changed two thousand years ago so that now the world is less of a mess than it was then? Do we really expect that the world will get better and better?

We can't help admiring people who work for change in the world. We cheer those who try to improve conditions. Habitat for Humanity, a wonderful organization, builds houses for poor people. The future homeowners themselves work on construction along with volunteers from all walks of life.

It is touching to see these volunteers, former President Jimmy Carter among them, hammering nails and sawing wood and making sure people have a decent place to live. It is wonderful to see people doing what they can to make the world a better place.

But if everyone had adequate housing, would that solve the problems of the world? In some cases, life actually becomes worse when your external circumstances improve.

I used to visit parts of England, and one of my ports of call was Manchester, a northern industrial town. I visited a woman who lived alone in a Manchester slum district. I marveled at how the neighbors would come and go from her house. Anyone on that street who had a problem would come to see her. When a child was born, she would act as a midwife or bring food. They called her the Mayor of Coronation Street because she was so involved in these people's lives.

In many ways, life in this district was pathetic. The housing was poor and the people had little income. But there was a positive spirit, and this woman was very much a part of it. After years of living in this slum, she was acknowledged for what she had done and was provided with government housing. She moved into a beautiful house. It was nice and clean.

When I visited her in her new house, I found her depressed and alone. She had nothing to do. She had no role in life and no one depended on her; there were no emergencies for her to look after. She would look out the window and see strangers walk by. She had an awful sense of guilt. She didn't feel she deserved that beautiful home. She died soon after that. In a way, it broke her heart to leave the slum.

In his book *The City of Joy* (1985), author Dominique Lapierre describes life in Calcutta, one of the largest slums on earth:

> Everything in these slums combined to drive their inhabitants to abjection and despair: shortage of work and chronic unemployment, appallingly low wages, the inevitable child labor, the impossibility of saving, debts that could never be redeemed, the mortgaging of personal possessions and their ultimate loss sooner or later. There was also the total nonexistence of any reserve food stocks and the necessity to buy in minute quantities—one cent's worth of salt, two or three cents' worth of wood, one match, a spoonful of sugar—and the total absence of privacy with ten or twelve people sharing a single room. Yet the miracle of these concentration camps was that the accumulation of disastrous elements was counterbalanced by other factors that allowed their inhabitants not merely to remain fully human but even to transcend their condition and become models of humanity.
>
> In these slums people actually put love and mutual support into practice. They knew how to be tolerant of all creeds and castes, how to give respect to a stranger, how to show charity toward beggars, cripples, lepers, and even the insane. Here the weak were helped, not trampled upon. Orphans were instantly adopted by their neighbors and old people were cared for and revered by their children.

These people lived in one of the world's worst areas, and yet they managed to "overcome the world."

We are inclined to blame circumstances for our internal state. I would be happy if only I had more money or a better house. But look at people who have what you long for, and ask them about the quality of their life. You will find that these things in themselves mean nothing for spiritual well-being.

At the world's finest restaurants, you can find people muttering about imperfect food or poor service. People can make misery out of the most exquisite surroundings. On the other hand, you can find people of scant means who share a simple loaf of bread with delight, as if it were the most delicious meal ever offered.

You have probably had the experience of visiting someone in the hospital, anticipating their pain and thinking, "I don't know how they can stand it"—and then you find that they cheer you up and that somehow they are faring well. They have overcome what seems unbearable to you, creating something that is beautiful and positive. They do not wait for the external world to change.

Overcoming the world means finding beauty even if the external situation is ugly. It means finding happiness whether you are wealthy or poor. It means experiencing that act of transformation in yourself—putting your will, effort, and attention into changing your experience of the world, rather than trying to change the world.

In every moment you can choose heaven or hell. You choose heaven by shifting your internal attitude, not by waiting for the external situation to change. If you wait for that, you will wait forever.

The world we need to overcome is the world in our own hearts. Any situation in your life can be transformed into a piece of heaven, depending on your own attitude and response.

And yet people are bound to make conditions: "Well, that's true if you are reasonably healthy and have enough money and a nice house, but what about . . . ?"

And people make exceptions: "What about torture? Could you experience heaven while being physically tortured?" Now doesn't that seem impossible? Who could experience heaven while locked up in jail and subjected to daily torment?

Yet we know there are people who have had exactly that experience and have come out transformed people. In some ways, they are almost thankful for what they went through because it challenged them to look to their internal life. Because the external situation was so horrible, they knew they were not going to find peace outside themselves, so they found it by going deeper within themselves.

Viktor Frankl, an Austrian neurologist and psychiatrist, was imprisoned in a Nazi concentration camp and lost most of his family; he transformed his experience and made of it a whole new approach to psychotherapy. Saint John of the Cross endured a long period in prison with frequent torture, yet it was there that he found his transformation; his tiny prison cell was where he found heaven.

Few of us go through such severe external pain, and yet we fuss about little things and believe they prevent our happiness. But the challenge is to *overcome* the world. You can choose not to let the external world dictate your internal attitude.

Trial is inevitable in our lives. The world is in a mess and we are bombarded with negative news. We need to remember that happiness does not depend on circumstances; we can choose how we let any circumstance affect our spiritual well-being. With help from our Higher Power, we can transform our inner state and overcome the world.

TOOLS FOR TASK 7

1. **Notice your response when an event or person causes you upset.** What emotions come to the forefront when the world seems too much to bear? Try turning to your Higher Power when you feel overwhelmed. Consider the possibility that your

Higher Power wants only the best for you and can help to lighten your burden.

2. **When you feel cut off from heaven, look inside yourself.** Do you notice that you want to wallow in your negativity? Try to connect with those deeper feelings of peace and serenity that help you deal calmly with the events of daily living.

3. **Check to see if an event that is dragging you down can be transformed.** You have an ability to transform how you view and react to this event in your life. Your happiness is not dependent on external circumstances. You have the ability to summon help from your Higher Power. Ask your Higher Power to help you view positive outcomes and best scenarios.

Participants Report on Task 7

TAMI: Last week I talked to a dear friend who lives in a different state. He was telling me about a situation with his brother. His brother had asked him, "Who put up the Christmas tree?" My friend explained that the brother who was asking had put the tree up, but couldn't remember doing it.

I felt myself get in concerned mode: Do I need to go to Missouri to give him support? Then this week's task came to mind, and I noticed that, even though it was a serious situation, my friend and his brother were able to be lighthearted and uplifting. It was a delight. It reminded me of how much their friendship meant to me, and I laughed and enjoyed the conversation.

My friend said he had decided to take his brother to the clinic for a checkup, and then he saw some EMTs along the way. It ended up that the EMTs took the brother to the hospital. They found out he had not had a stroke but possibly a blood clot. Throughout the story, both he and his brother were joking the whole time.

That set the mood for me for the week, and it showed me how the universe teaches us lessons whether we want to learn them or not. I was not very attentive to our task for the week. Then, rather than me practicing it, my friends' situation forced the practice onto me because *they* were doing the task.

I always feel like angels work in my life like that; they bring things to me. I felt like that was an angel's blessing. I was able to see that situation and not be so devastated, because they weren't devastated. They had transformed the situation with laughter.

BOB: I didn't think I was going to have to work this task. I felt that my life is so good that I didn't need it.

But Michael reminded us recently that overcoming little things is as important to your spiritual well-being as working to overcome the big things. He also reminded me that little health issues are not insignificant to a person worried about his physical well-being.

I will start my story by saying that I was working on overcoming something that was pretty significant to me. About four months ago, I came off the golf course and sat down at a restaurant with my golf buddies. I reached out to grab a glass of water and could not pick up the glass with either hand! Immediately, my buddies checked my pupils. They made me walk on a line, listened to my speech, and reviewed all the things you are supposed to check for heart attack and stroke symptoms.

In a few minutes, the strength returned so I figured I must have pinched a nerve. But it happened four more times over the next two months, and I started to get concerned about it. Sometimes it would be as simple as playing one hole of golf and then I could not pick up the putter. These symptoms were bilateral and symmetrical—based on my online research, this ruled out stroke and heart attack and so did all the other symptoms. So I thought, big deal, it's just a pinched nerve.

The fifth time it happened, my sweetheart told me I needed to see the doctor. My doctor was upset with me. After examining me, she sent me for carotid artery sonograms to make sure nothing had busted loose and gotten into the part of my brain where it could affect both arms. She referred me to a neurologist for an MRI.

All this time I was pushing this into the background, thinking it was no big deal, that it was just a transient thing. I was not going to let it affect me. But it ate at me. It started coming to a head this week, after I showed up at the neurologist's office thinking he would simply review my symptoms and send me for an MRI.

But no! An hour and fifteen minutes later, after being attached to all kinds of electrodes and having shocks sent through my body, I began to get a little worried. The neurologist said everything was normal in my arms. I had some carpal tunnel that was mild. He scheduled an MRI and gave me a whole list of lab tests. I agreed to do the fifteen tests because he wanted to check for three diseases that could cause my symptoms. It made me think that his concern went well beyond a pinched nerve!

This week's task came to mind. I had been doing really well about ignoring this and overcoming it. But I needed to get a handle on this new information. So today I had the lab tests. I had to go to four different laboratories. It was not a pleasant experience. I had to give seven vials out of one arm and two out of the other.

Suddenly my mind started to let the beasts out of the basement and I had something to work on. I needed to transform the event.

How could I transform the "fear" beast? I was worried because a great deal of who I am, and a lot of my social life, is based on playing sports. I want to keep being active as long as I can.

Here is what I resolved this afternoon: after meditating and praying for a while, I thought that this task had come along at the right time. How do I transform the event? I need to remember that it is probably nothing but a bone spur or inflammation of arthritis. In ninety percent of cases, according to my Internet research, that is what causes these symptoms.

I tried to change my thoughts, from worry to "Isn't it wonderful that now I am being looked at by all these people? They are ruling out all these other problems!"

So this can be an opportunity not to be afraid of the outcome but to welcome the outcome. I can view it as an opportunity to see if there really is something I need to worry about. Unfortunately, it will be months before all these tests are completed. So in the meantime, I will work on transforming the situation into a positive opportunity!

I ASK MYSELF, "WHAT IS THE LESSON I AM MISSING? WHAT FEARS ARE NAGGING AT ME?"

BETSY: I had some physical challenges too. I have had arthritis for many years, and in the last five days I have dealt with a lot of pain.

So much of what I normally deal with is left over from a ravage of arthritis years ago. Fatigue is one of the biggest effects, but I am still trying to do everything I've always done at Christmastime. If I looked at it realistically, it would just seem absurd. My body is telling me that things are changing. My mind is going to have to change on how I view this. I have the same challenge as Bob: the fear sneaks in. The fear beast asks, "Is this what I am going to be dealing with from now on?"

I am pretty good at dealing with my level of pain. I have an extremely high pain threshold. I pack my life full as a distraction. But I have not been able to be distracted from this period of pain. So I may need to rise to a new level. I ask myself, "What is the lesson I am missing? What fears are nagging at me?"

One of the fears is: Who am I if I cannot do all the things I used to do? People don't see me only for what I do, so why do I identify so much with what I do?

Maybe the lesson is to learn how to ask for help. I asked my son for help ordering some things online, because it hurts if I am at the computer too long. He was so tender and sweet about doing it. If I had not asked, I would have missed that whole opportunity.

So in learning how to ask for what I need, I learned not to identify myself with what I can or cannot do.

Part of the Christmas story, in my mind, is how tenderly the shepherds take care of their sheep. I need to be more of a shepherd to

"OVERCOMING THE WORLD" IS LIKE GOING UP
FROM THE BASEMENT . . . AND SEEING LIFE DIFFERENTLY.

myself, and I am not good at that; I plow through and deny the pain. I do what I need to do and quietly deal with it.

I try to remember the possibility that God may use your struggle to bring you something magnificent.

Many years ago, I hiked twelve miles into a beautiful Arizona canyon. I always dreamed of going back, but I was having trouble with my knees. So I set returning to the canyon as a goal and went through a lot of steps toward that. I realized that knee replacements would have to be a part of that process. I had two knee replacements.

Our son, as a surprise for his dad's birthday and a gift for me, organized an all-adult family trip to the canyon. It turned out more magnificent than anything I could have dreamed of. But the dream had started out as part of a struggle. I think overcoming the world can be a beautiful thing if God is part of it.

I know this week's task is asking me to rise to a higher level and learn something. Part of me just wants to do things exactly the way I always have and fill my life to overflowing. I have so much resistance, but it is obvious that I need to change. This was a good task for me. I am staring change and struggle in the face and cannot ignore it; I have to learn from it.

MICHAEL: The world has seemed very large, and I keep trying to come to grips with the world and transform my experience of it. Is this what it means to be "in the world but not of the world"?

I am in the world but not of all my life circumstances. They are not who I am. I am not going with the flow, being at peace with the world; I am often in the midst of chaos.

What is it exactly that we are to overcome? My bottom line on that is that I must transform every moment, to be ready and able to transform whatever is supposed to happen next. Perhaps it is like leaving this world and going to the next. Or maybe it is as simple as going to the grocery store; whatever is going to be the transformation in the moment. Just sitting here can transform me, because sharing other people's experiences then starts my own process going.

I remember walking into the oncologist's office five years ago, thinking, "Well, I will either get a death sentence, treatment, or a clean bill of health." And that is how I transformed the experience: instead of just sitting in the chair thinking the worst, I knew there were three options and whatever it is, it is! And so, every six months, those are my options—and this has transformed the whole experience for me.

Here is a poem I wrote about it:

> Listen, My Fellow Spiritual Travelers, dark though it may be,
> We are saying thank you from the bottom of our hearts.
> Thank you for our freedoms and for your undying love,
> Thank you for all the people who care and want the world to be a better place.
> With the rainforest disappearing and global warming melting the icecaps,
> We are saying thank you for our beautiful planet.

With the landfills overflowing and the fish disappearing from the oceans,
We are saying thank you for the abundance of the earth.
With the bombs falling and people dying,
We are saying thank you for life.
With soldiers dying and wounds to body, mind and spirit,
We are saying thank you for their courage and dedication to duty.
With the abyss staring us in the face,
We are saying thank you for all Your benefits towards us.
All life is precious and, dark though it is, with terror ruling the night,
We stand on the brink of light and our hearts are filled with love.

KITTY: I want to share this thought about overcoming the world: Looking down from a high hill at a tempestuous sea is a super visual picture for me. I am working very hard not to be judgmental.

The clerk at the market this week was harried with the volume of shoppers. She seemed annoyed that I was taking too long to empty my cart. I took a deep breath and said, "I'll hurry, but you take a well-deserved deep breath too." She turned and said, "Thank you for caring." Boy that was an instantaneous result! I left the market with a big smile!

LEADER: When life hands us those inevitable challenges and changes, we have choices about how we adapt. I think that's what this task is talking about. When you get thrown something in your life, you have choices about how to react to it.

Transforming the event can help you pull yourself out of a negative state and into a heavenly state. If spiritual growth has taught me nothing else, it has taught me that there is always an alternative once you become aware of where you are. Discovering this has transformed my life.

JACK: My family has a core of four people for our Christmas dinner: my wife, me, my brother, and my son. For the last six or seven years, we have taken in an occasional "stray," and it has become one of the central parts of Christmas that we look forward to the most. This year we are going to have five "waifs and strays" who would otherwise have nowhere to go. Actually, I'm sure they would find something to do, but we like to think that being in a family-like setting for Christmas is a good thing. It certainly is for us, and we intend for it to be for them. Their presence lifts me up and makes me forget the stress of the holiday.

WE STAND ON THE BRINK OF LIGHT AND OUR HEARTS ARE FILLED WITH LOVE.

LEADER: "Overcoming the world" is like going up from the basement, walking up the stairs and seeing life differently. We open up to the possibilities of what God might be teaching us. Sometimes the result is so much better than anything you could have imagined, that it takes your breath away.

Enrichment Reading

1. These things I have spoken to you, that in Me you may have peace. In the world you will have tribulation; but be of good cheer, I have overcome the world. (John 16:33)

2. Those who are conscious of the Lord's presence perceive that each and all things that happen to them do them some good, and that evil never touches them; as a result they are calm. (Emanuel Swedenborg, *Secrets of Heaven* 5963)

3. When our beliefs and life are filled with deep truth, we are in the Lord's kingdom and in a calm state, at which point we view external matters the way a person on a towering hill observes the sea heaving below. (Emanuel Swedenborg, *Secrets of Heaven* 4394)

4. I am not asking you to take them out of the world, but I ask you to protect them from the evil one. They do not belong to the world, just as I do not belong to the world. (John 17:15,16)

5. Work on yourself can have marvelous results. . . . The Work is to transform your relations to life. All the practical things said in it have this object. This is to *work on oneself*. . . . What is your task? Why are you down here? What is it that you have to change? What is it that you have to learn about yourself, this thing you take for granted, this thing that is your apparatus for living? Does your apparatus for living give you the results you wish for? . . . And that means working on yourself and your mechanical reactions to all that happens. For your mechanical reactions to life are *yourself* and that makes your unhappiness. . . . Try to think that it is not life you can change, but yourself in your reaction to life. This is where the first idea of what it means to work on oneself lies. Once you see the idea, then, whatever the conditions of life, you have a power in your grasp whose value is beyond price. You have begun to grasp the pearl, to see what life on earth really means. (Maurice Nicoll, *Psychological Commentaries on the Teaching of Gurdjieff and Ouspensky,* vol. 1)

Task 8

GO UPSTAIRS TO PRAY

 When you pray, remember that you are a spiritual being, in the light of your Higher Power. Raise your awareness to the highest level of your "house."

- Try to see what you are praying about from the viewpoint of your Higher Power.
- Pray for wisdom and insight to see the spiritual truth of the situation.
- Ask for the courage and ability to make choices and take actions that your Higher Power leads you to see.

Learning Objectives

- *Practice being open to the influx of love and wisdom from your Higher Power.*
- *Practice feeling the true meaning of your prayer.*
- *Understand that gratitude can open your connection to your Higher Power.*
- *Learn to pray about yourself last.*

Do you feel that all of your prayers are answered? Jesus said, "Whatever you ask for in prayer with faith, you will receive" (Matthew 21:22). But if we feel our prayers are not answered, we may develop serious doubts about our faith. Let's look at some reasons why prayers do not seem to be answered.

One reason is that mechanical prayers are not answered. These prayers are just words. You know in Shakespeare's *Hamlet*, where Hamlet is about to kill the king, but he cannot do it while the king is praying? Hamlet is afraid that if he kills the king during prayer, the king would go straight to heaven. Then you find that the king is saying, "My words fly up, my thoughts remain below. Words without thoughts never to heaven go." So he wasn't really praying at all.

There are prayers that are just words, like a mumbling prayer when we don't really know what we are praying about. Often we are like the child who goes to the parent and hems and haws, standing on one foot, then the other, until finally the parent asks, "What do you want?" The child does not know, so the parent says, "Come back when you know." Until you are clear on the intent of your prayer, how can you expect an answer?

Another barrier to prayer being answered is conflict—a lack of correspondence between our prayer and our actions, like when a person prays for good health but does things that are unhealthy. If you are serious about your prayer, show it with your actions and not only with your prayers. The old saying, "Actions speak louder than words," applies to prayer as well.

I remember a time when I had trouble with a frozen shoulder, and I was conscious that I was not praying about it. Finally, I thought perhaps I ought to pray about it. When I did, it became clear to me that I could not just say, "Well, I prayed about it and I don't need to do anything else." I needed to take action.

Part of my difficulty was that I did not know what the appropriate action was. In the end, I was led to a solution that worked, but I had avoided praying about it because I did not want to do what prayer might have told me to do.

You know the saying, "Be careful what you pray for, because you might get it"? Well, there is also a saying, "Be careful what you pray for, because you might get an answer you don't want to hear."

Ill will is another barrier to prayers being answered. Psalm 66 says, "If I had cherished iniquity in my heart, the Lord would not have listened." And in the New Testament: "When you are offering your gift at the altar, if you remember that your brother or sister has something against you, leave your gift there before the altar and go; first be reconciled to your brother or sister, and then come and offer your gift" (Matthew 23,24). Don't make the offering until you are reconciled, and then you can offer your prayer out of a clear heart with good will.

There are some prayers that we don't realize have an element of ill will. Have you ever prayed that you would win the lottery? Would that imply that someone else should not win the lottery? Or consider the person who hears fire sirens and prays, "Dear God, don't let it be my house!" Does that mean it should be the neighbor's house? I guess we could pray for a false alarm. But there are times that we pray for a personal outcome that, if it were realized, would hurt someone else. Such prayers are not heard.

For this task, we want to focus particularly on prayers that are too external or too short-term, where we ask on a different level than the Lord answers. This can apply to prayer for ourselves as well as to prayer for others.

Here's an example. I know someone who prayed for a certain car. I think it was a red Buick. He got this car but it was a lemon. The problem was that his prayer was too external.

Here's a more challenging one. Imagine you have a friend in the hospital. Do you pray for your friend to become well? Suppose it is that person's time to die? Do you really want your prayer to override the appropriate next step in your friend's life?

So if you pray for yourself or for others on too external a level, as if you know what is best, then you are going to dislike the answer. Or you would not want the prayer to be answered.

The Bible teaches that when you pray, you should go into your closet. Guess where the closet is. It's upstairs, on the highest level of your spiritual house. Get as high in your house as you can when you pray. Then see what happens to your prayers.

Think on as deep a level as you can about your prayer, and see if that changes the feeling of the prayer. What are you really praying about? What do you truly expect out of the prayer?

When doing this task, I found myself praying about the expansion of our church facilities. What happens when you pray from a high level about something like that? I couldn't pray that we get our new building within a year, because maybe that's the wrong timing. Or that it be a certain size—maybe that's wrong for our future needs. When I sent my prayer to a higher level, the prayer changed; instead of praying for a specific outcome, I could pray, "Whatever happens, let us approach this in a way that is in the spirit of your kingdom." Because maybe we get what we pray for, but everybody gets so mad at each other that the whole thing falls apart anyway.

Lift your prayer to a high level and you find that the nature of your prayer changes. The power of prayer grows when you raise your awareness as close as possible to your Higher Power, so that your prayer is in that spirit.

Here is the amazing thing: prayer really comes into us from above. Often we think prayer comes from outside, from circumstances, but it's the prayer that comes into our hearts from our Higher Power that is really answered. But first you have to rise to a high enough level to see what that prayer is.

What is the essence of the thing we pray for? It is hard to let go of your own external will, which is accustomed to demanding its own way. It can be like a difficult negotiation. It's hard to let go of your will and say to your Higher Power, "It is your divine will that counts."

TOOLS FOR TASK 8

1. **Open your prayer to the highest part of yourself.** When you get into the higher part of your mind when you pray, you approach your Higher Power from the best part of yourself. Let your prayer express your higher self and all the love and charity in your highest levels. Pray with awareness that the love of your Higher Power can transform events and improve your state of mind. This is what is meant by "God's will be done."

2. **Allow gratitude to be part of your prayer.** Start your prayer with thanks for your blessings. A grateful spirit can open your communication with your Higher Power. Your prayer then comes from the highest level of your spiritual self.

3. **When you pray, take time to listen for an answer.** Do you know how prayer is answered? Neither does anyone else, but one thing is certain: if you don't open yourself to receive an answer, you will never receive one. Find a quiet spot to pray. Then, with open awareness, journal freely about whatever comes to mind. Often the thoughts you write down contain the answer you are seeking.

Participants Report on Task 8

BETSY: I have accepted that most of my learning is a spiral ladder. The same challenge keeps coming around, many times over. Each time I am asked to see it from a higher point of view and with more clarity.

Learning to pray includes a vertical dimension, but it also seems fluid, and at times just out of reach. When I recognize that I expect to feel more connected afterwards to God, I realize that instant results are not part of his eternal vision. I remind myself that prayer is a journey—sometimes easy, sometimes difficult.

I've observed some factors that contribute or hinder my "success" with prayer:

1. Quiet, undisturbed place.
2. My willingness to spend time with God.
3. My ability to lift my mind out and up from my daily concerns.
4. My ability to place my attention on the God in me, felt as my breath.
5. My ability to come to the Lord with gratitude and a willingness to listen to what he wants from me.
6. My ability to look within myself and to God for answers, and not blame others or resist.

This month my prayers have been filled with gratitude. It is as if God has opened my mind and heart to see all the blessings I have been given. Thanking him is the first step. As my response, I want to live a grateful life with joy and positive thoughts. I want to make it my responsibility to be happy and pass that happiness on to others.

The second part of my prayers this month has been wrestling with change: physical, emotional, and spiritual change. I want to learn to accept it, to be grateful in the moment and aware that there will be change in the future. Change is inevitable.

Growth demands change. It's hard to step forward and circle up that spiral ladder. I move from the comfort of the familiar to a new place. It takes effort, but God has a plan for me and I must be willing to reach out and embrace a new era of my life. So I pray that I face change with courage and confidence, knowing he will be by my side.

LEYLA: First a quote from Mahatma Gandhi: "If we have listening ears, God speaks to us in our own language, whatever that language be."

By "language," I think of all the ways we perceive and interpret. Many of my prayers come as an internal dialog about what I see and experience. An example: I talk to God internally by saying things like "Isn't that a beautiful grouping of flowers?" My feelings while observing the flowers are of awe and peace. These are certainly gifts from God.

I might have a dialog about wanting to see something differently, to allow an opening to better communication. If I'm in a still place in my mind, I might verbalize this more directly to God. I then open myself up to find the guidance I seek. I think the way you receive answers to prayers is always miraculous.

I have great faith that God communicates with me on my own level. I try not to sweat the small stuff about what form my prayers might take. Invariably, when I reach out to God, he finds me! He even finds me through the muddied water of my life—but I have to be looking and listening.

KITTY: Facing the first Christmas without my son was a challenge. Turning to prayer was soothing and gave me the courage to tackle ornaments, pictures, decorations, and even the named stockings with more love than anger at my loss.

When tears were near, I prayed (talked) to my God and asked for courage and acceptance that my son was in a good place. Prayers took me to a healthy place of cherished memories and gave me a trust that God was with me.

I prayed for enlightenment to see the situation spiritually, and I meditated to focus on being a spiritual being. I am truly losing the self-pity that has haunted me. I pray for the strength to see things as they are in God's eyes and to stay connected to him.

HERB: I accidentally learned how to pray years ago while lying in a rice paddy. The situation was bad; I prayed for help and let go of my emotions. Just for an instant I was very comfortable within myself as I prayed. After things quieted down, I realized what had happened.

I have prayed that way ever since. I have even gotten to the point of doing it when saying the Lord's Prayer in church. Up to that point the Lord's Prayer was something I had learned to repeat by rote.

LEADER: When you feel like you are only repeating the Lord's Prayer by rote, read through the translation* that we use in our sessions. This new translation from the original Greek text is a great tool to help us think about what we are praying and to see the deeper meaning of the prayer, rather than just repeat phrases from memory.

I AM TRULY LOSING THE SELF-PITY THAT HAS HAUNTED ME.

TAMI: I think of myself as an emotional person. I often cry when I have a conscious thought about God and the blessings he has given me.

I'm overwhelmingly grateful for anything that happens in my life. Once I had an accident that totaled my vehicle. Upon telling my story "enthusiastically" to a friend, he said, "You seem excited and happy that you had a wreck!" I said, "Yes, indeed, I am! The angels protected me and I didn't even have to go to the hospital. I wasn't even harmed!"

I've always believed that our inner thoughts are a block to all of our relationships, including our relationship with God. When we can divert our runaway thoughts with a focus (usually through meditation), this helps to unblock that two-way communication with God.

Other diversions can open the communication as well. Perhaps we tune in a radio station to listen to music while driving. Then we

*See translation of the Lord's Prayer on page 135.

may hear a song that reminds us of a loved one who died years ago. This is another example of how God works in our lives.

When I practice feeling God's presence, I ask, "Does this feel right within my heart?" The answer I get has never been wrong. It is a feeling from within that I have learned to trust.

I believe that God knows our truth. God knows what is in our hearts. It is up to us to practice knowing what lies in our own heart. I try to do that through prayer.

JACK: Learning how to pray is a big subject. These days, partly as a result of this group and partly as a result of other work I've been doing, I worry less about both the form and the content of my prayers. Instead, my goal is to make an effort to make contact with God by sitting down at a set time each day.

My prayer session starts with a few memorized prayers and moves into a silent meditation. Most days it goes for a half hour. I assume each time that I will receive exactly what I should from each session. I attempt to adopt an attitude that I am simply not in charge.

Even when I have been sure that I had a solid, conscious contact with God, I don't dwell on it, though I do take some time to enjoy it and may recall it later, especially when I see challenges looming. Instead, I notice how things that used to frustrate me aren't as frustrating, or how things that used to frighten me aren't as frightening.

Of course when I backslide, either by not finding the time for spiritual practice or by missing a few sessions, I assume that it's part of the learning process. My job is to "keep on keeping on" and not to give up the spiritual practices.

The second thing I try to do is notice positive results and feelings, with the emphasis less on the actual meditation experience and more on the gradual change in my attitude. I look for change in my spiritual condition over time.

VICKY: I do not know how I would get by day to day without prayer. With my health and emotional challenges, the only way I know how to deal is through prayer.

I start and end my day with prayer—talking to God, not just learned prayers or automatic words. I have been doing this for so long that I would not be able to function without prayer.

WHEN I REACH OUT TO GOD, HE FINDS ME! HE EVEN FINDS ME THROUGH THE MUDDIED WATER OF MY LIFE.

JULIE: I request strength to remember to connect daily. I ask blessings for us all, that we may feel the angels nudging us and remember to follow our heart and intuition. I become blocked when I get in a rush.

How ironic! I become irritated with myself when I realize late in the day that I haven't taken any time that day to connect with the Divine. I've felt answers, yet I keep attempting to "steer the boat." I must continue trying to flow with the river rather than fight it.

I do feel connected to God, especially when I take some quiet time to reflect and be grateful. Nature always helps me to do this quickly. Have you seen how many things are in bloom here in Tucson in the first week of February? What a treat it is. It's a sure sign of heaven on earth to me.

I continue to strive for an attitude of openness. I feel I am in the right place when I remember that. But then I'm right back to "steering the boat"! I'm extremely grateful when I can see all the blessings in my life. Spiritual growth groups, church, and angels sending earthly messengers really help me remain open and forever grateful.

BOB: I'm back from Texas with a fresh grandbaby fix. They wore me out!

Since my predominant activity for the last few weeks has been driving, I decided to give some thought to spiritual growth while on the road.

Many of you know that some years ago I was involved in a rear-end collision. A truck driver talking on a cell hit me from the rear while I was stopped at a red light.

I never heard her coming, because she never applied the brakes. The trauma (mostly mental) still haunts me. The sound of my car crushing around me from the rear is still fresh in my memory.

So what does this have to do with learning how to pray? For this task, I decided to examine my attitude toward driving and to pray for enlightenment and some relief from the stress I've endured since that accident years ago.

When I prayed for understanding, I asked God to reveal to me what is really happening to my inner being when I encounter a rude or careless driver on the road. I asked for understanding of my stressful reaction when I encounter heavy and pressing traffic. I asked for patience to replace stress. I asked for calm to replace anger.

The answer came in the realization that I am afraid when I drive. The trauma of that accident years ago is still in the forefront of my mind!

IT IS UP TO US TO PRACTICE KNOWING WHAT LIES IN OUR OWN HEART.

The answer also came in my realization that I know some techniques for defensive driving: observing other drivers and road conditions, using distance to separate myself from potential danger, avoiding distractions both in and outside the car. Perhaps these techniques can help make me less fearful and more confident behind the wheel.

Finally, I realized that I really enjoy driving when I don't feel threatened. I love my old car and the feel of the highway under my tires. I revel in understanding the mechanics that make the machine perform so well to my touch. I repeated a prayer of gratitude for those things I like about the experience on the road.

So here I am, asking God to help me deal with yet another of the negatives in my life. Perhaps that is what spiritual growth is all about.

MICHAEL: I have two things I learned about prayer and praying. First, the Lord has already implanted the prayer in our hearts; it is our task to have the prayer come into our thoughts and be expressed. And, real prayer commands action; prayer without action is no prayer at all.

I often use this method for praying. I find that I typically say the Lord's Prayer or the Twenty-third Psalm. I tried a new method of praying by asking: What am I praying for? Who am I praying about? When do I pray? Where do I pray? Why do I pray? I found that the results were different every time I did this. It was interesting to write down some of the results.

I ATTEMPT TO ADOPT AN ATTITUDE THAT I AM SIMPLY NOT IN CHARGE.

When listening for any answer to my prayers, I turned to the Bible. I think I get my answers when I read the Bible. I don't hear voices or see lights; rather, sometimes I will get a thought and then ask myself, "That's interesting, where did that come from?"

I have this feeling of being connected to a Higher Power. I find that each time I remember to pray, there is a shift in my state of mind; prayer takes me away from worry and anxiety, and it reminds me that I am connected to my Creator, the source of all good and truth.

LEADER: This is a wonderful task. Each of us took time to examine our connection with our Higher Power. And we each saw how prayer helps open us to view our life experience from a higher perspective. By using our ability to communicate (including our listening skills) in prayer and meditation, we have brought our minds into the highest level of the house, where peace and love reside. Praying from a higher perspective does a great deal to keep those beasts in the basement of our minds.

Enrichment Reading

1. But whenever you pray, go into your room and shut the door and pray to your Father who is in secret; and your Father who sees in secret will reward you. (Matthew 6:6)

2. Every time I say the Lord's prayer, I plainly perceive that I am rising up toward the Lord as if I am being drawn toward him. Then my ideas open up, and as a result a communication is brought about with some communities in heaven; and I notice that the Lord flows into every detail of the prayer, and therefore into every idea in my thought that is from the meaning of the things in the prayer. This inflow occurs with indescribable variety, and is never the same from one time to the next. This shows that the details in the prayer contain an infinity of things, and that the Lord is present in every one of them. (Emanuel Swedenborg, *Secrets of Heaven* 6476)

3. Regarded in itself, praying is talking with God, while taking an inward view of the things we are praying about. In answer we receive a similar stream of speech into the perceptions or thoughts of our mind, so that there is some opening of our inner self to God. The experience varies, depending on our mood and the nature of the subject we are praying about. If we pray from love and faith and focus on or seek only what is heavenly and spiritual, something resembling a revelation emerges while we pray. It discloses itself in our emotions in the form of hope, comfort, or an inward stirring of joy. (Emanuel Swedenborg, *Secrets of Heaven* 2535)

KEEP CHOOSING JOY

Our spiritual growth program is based on a simple premise: our Higher Power wishes us to experience peace, joy, tranquility, and love in our lives. In our group work, we have learned that this can be accomplished only by taming the demands of our ego. Ego-based self-love runs counter to the happiness our Higher Power wants for us.

When we become aware that negatives and evils are invading our lives, we can use the techniques we've learned in this program. We can open ourselves to see the choices in each moment. We can let peace and love flow into our lives.

Spiritual work is not easy. Effort is required. We must first become aware of the negatives and evils that are affecting us, and then we must choose how we react to those invading negatives.

Our Higher Power allows us to choose how we react to our everyday lives. We can choose how we let people, situations, and events affect our state of mind and our spiritual well-being.

Here are some of the most effective strategies we have found to help integrate spiritual growth and joy into our everyday lives.

HAVE GRATITUDE
Gratitude is a critical element of spiritual growth. With gratitude, we remember that life is essentially good, despite its pains and problems, and that we are loved by a Higher Power who showers us with blessings. Sometimes we are too wrapped up in day-to-day concerns to

reflect on these blessings. One of the best ways we can reconnect with our Higher Power and support our own growth is to reflect on the things for which we are grateful.

RELAX

Our body tensions seem to support negativity. When our muscles are tight and tense, it is hard for our inner spiritual self to relax and go with the flow of life. Physical relaxation is one of the most important aids that our group's members have found to support their spiritual development.

CULTIVATE LOVING RELATIONSHIPS

People are created not to live alone, but to live in loving relationship with others. These relationships may form with family, friends, work companions, or others who are working on their spiritual journey. Loving relationships are the real-life laboratory where we learn what it is to be spiritual.

ENJOY BEAUTY

Natural beauty is a great teacher. There is nothing like fresh air and beautiful surroundings to lift our spirits. By the millions, people flock to national parks and places of beauty. It is as if we instinctively know that beauty is a gift to the soul.

READ INSPIRATIONAL AND DEVOTIONAL LITERATURE

The mind is like a garden that thrives on cultivation: we human beings need a rich flow of inspirational thoughts coming into our minds. It is easy to rely too much on the news and entertainment media for this kind of input. To cultivate our best selves, many people find it helpful to spend a few moments each day reading and meditating on some spiritual message, whether from the Bible or some other source of inspiration.

MEDITATE

Meditation can take many forms. What they all have in common is some manner of discipline to still our conscious levels of thinking, opening the way for deeper perception and insight. Using our analogy of the house, daily meditation is like telling the animals in your basement to be quiet for just a few minutes, while you listen for what might be going on higher in your house.

SHARE YOUR JOURNEY WITH A FRIEND OR GROUP

The power of spiritual work is even greater when we share our experience with another person or with a group. The group materials provided in the appendix can be used for conducting your own spiritual growth group.

PERFORM ACTS OF KINDNESS

There is tremendous value in stopping to notice the needs of others, and in doing what we can to fill those needs. Think of the people in your life. Is someone going through a difficult time? Is an anniversary coming up? Do you sense that anyone in your life could do with some help or encouraging words? Performing acts of kindness is a gift to others, and it can give your spiritual life a boost.

BE USEFUL

Life is a vast and complex functional system, each person serving others and being served by others. Each human being is a part of this marvelous system of interlocking functions. We are each here to benefit from it and also to serve and support it. Performing useful tasks reminds us that we are contributing members of the human race.

PRAY

Prayer, at the heart of spiritual life, is communication and reconnection with our Higher Power. A spiritual life is a life in connection with the source of our being. It is a life in which we try to align our-selves with the flow of the universe. In prayer we express gratitude for blessings received. We ask for support in living a spiritual life. We open ourselves to receive our Higher Power's guidance and love. Most members of our group include prayer in their life every day.

REMEMBER THE LEVELS OF YOUR HOUSE

When we work on our spiritual well-being, it is helpful to keep our model of the mind in our thoughts.

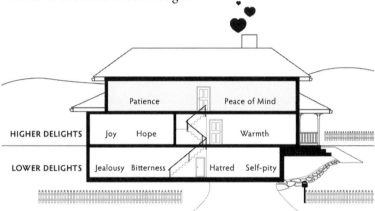

Emanuel Swedenborg describes the human mind as a three-level house:

> The human mind is divided into three regions. From our highest region we focus on God; from our second or middle region we focus on the world; and from our third or lowest region we focus on ourselves. Because our mind has this structure, it can be lifted up or can lift itself up to focus on God and heaven; it can be spread out or spread itself out in every direction to focus on the world and its nature; and it can be lowered down or can lower itself down to focus on the earth and hell. In these respects physical sight emulates mental sight—physical sight too can look up, around, and down.
>
> The human mind is like a three-story house with stairs that provide tran-sitions between levels. There are angels from heaven living on the top floor, people of the world on the middle floor, and demons on the bottom floor.

People for whom these three categories of love have been prioritized in the right way can go up or down whenever they want. . . .

When these three categories of love are properly prioritized in us, they are also coordinated in such a way that the highest love, our love for heaven, is present in the second love, our love for the world, and through that in the third or lowest love, our love for ourselves. In fact, the love that is inside steers the love that is outside wherever it wants. Therefore if a love for heaven is present in our love for the world and through that in our love for ourselves, with each type of love we accomplish useful things that are inspired by the God of heaven. . . . If these three loves are prioritized in the right way, they improve us, but if they are not prioritized in the right way, they damage us and turn us upside down. (Emanuel Swedenborg, *True Christianity* 395)

This model helps each of us choose which level of the mind we will inhabit. We make this choice every day, over and over, because the only time we can choose positive growth is in the present moment.

Thank you for participating with us in this worthwhile endeavor.

APPENDIX:
TOOLS FOR SPIRITUAL GROWTH GROUPS

ALL THE TASKS

Task 1: Explore the Levels of Your House

For this first week, focus on the human mind as a "house of spiritual aware-ness." When you experience an emotion, take a moment to notice on which level of your "house" the emotion resides.

- If you discover that your emotion resides in the lower levels of your "house," see if your awareness, by itself, shines enough light on that "beast in your basement" to lessen its impact on your spiritual well-being.

- When you experience a negative emotion, reflect on parts of your life that you experience in a higher, more joyful place. See if your thoughts of more joyful experience bring peace to replace the negative focus of your thoughts.

- Journal about your experience with this task.

- For groups: Come to your next group meeting prepared to share the impact of any new awareness you have experienced.

Task 2: Raise Your Mind

Once a day, practice raising your mind to a higher level.

- You can use this task to deal with a negative emotion—to rise above anger, fear, resentment, etc.

- You can practice this task in relation to another person—raising your mind to see him or her from an angelic point of view.

- You may use this task in relation to religious study or contemplation of nature, elevating your mind to see scripture or nature in the light of heaven. What is the message here from your Higher Power?

- You might use this task in relation to a particular event or circumstance in your life. How does that event or situation look in relation to your eternal life story?

Task 3: Stop Taking Credit

Observe your lower nature trying to take credit for what you say and do.

- You may notice resentment in your lower nature because you are not getting sufficient recognition or praise.

- You may observe a certain pleasure and self-satisfaction when you are praised.

- When you become conscious of one of these states, say in your heart: "This praise does not belong to me. Give God the praise." Then observe any change in yourself.

Task 4: Be Useful

Every day this week, make a conscious effort to put yourself out for the sake of the common good.

- Do at least one thing each day that takes you out of concern for yourself to concern for the welfare of others.

- While doing this task, notice any negative state that comes up for you.

Task 5: Let Go of Rushing

Observe yourself rushing, and experiment with letting go of the need to rush.

- Notice the physical and emotional symptoms you have when you are rushing. Observe the thoughts that justify your condition of haste, and test to see if those thoughts are correct.

- Notice what you were doing before feeling rushed, and what you do afterward.

- Experiment with letting go of these feelings, separating your higher self from your irrational, emotional self. Use the affirmation: "It is rushing, but I don't have to."

Task 6: Stop Giving Advice

Spend the next twenty-four hours observing your impulse to give advice, directly or indirectly. After that first day of self-observation, stop giving advice for a whole week.

- Keep in mind that you are doing this task for the sake of your own spiritual growth, and not to deprive other people of your wisdom.

- If for some reason you feel you must give advice, do so only from a higher place in yourself.

Task 7: Overcome the World

When you are upset by some event, situation, or person, and you wish things would change, turn your attention inward and upward.

- Change the context of your experience so that you find its positive value.

- Transform the situation.

Task 8: Go Upstairs to Pray

When you pray, remember that you are a spiritual being, in the light of your Higher Power. Raise your awareness to the highest level of your "house."

- Try to see what you are praying about from the viewpoint of your Higher Power.

- Pray for wisdom and insight to see the spiritual truth of the situation.

- Ask for the courage and ability to make choices and take actions that your Higher Power leads you to see.

Continuing Spiritual Growth

For your group's final meeting, we suggest that participants come prepared to discuss not only Task 8 but their total spiritual growth experience. This is also a good session to discuss where the group would like to go from this point.

The Arizona Spiritual Growth Foundation offers a great deal of material for spiritual growth work, including readings, recordings, and many more spiritual growth tasks. See "More Resources" on page 136.

FUNCTIONS OF A GROUP LEADER

1. Keep the discussion within preset time limits.

2. Listen carefully with mind and heart to what is said.

3. Observe what is going on in the group.

4. Protect the group from domination by self or by others, and stifle crosstalk.

5. Pay attention to the needs and interest of all participants.

6. Encourage and welcome participation from those who are reticent.

7. Allow all opinions to be heard.

8. Make it easy and comfortable for participants to speak.

9. Allow questions and responsibility to be handled by the group, and not only by the leader.

10. Encourage discussion that focuses on the here and now, and on each participant in the present moment.

11. Set an example of openness and honesty in communication.

12. Create an atmosphere of trust and caring.

SAMPLE SESSION OUTLINE

Task 1: Explore the Levels of Your House

Setup: Music background, chairs with notebooks, subdued lighting.

Welcome: Welcome and introduce leader (and co-leader).

Introductions: Go around the group and ask participants to introduce themselves by answering three questions:

- What is your name?
- How are you?
- What brought you here?

Meditation: Talk about the use of meditation to center the group and to focus our attention on our inner being. Use a guided meditation to set the mood.

Handouts: Group Guidelines and the new version of the Lord's Prayer. Explain that this is a translation from Luke's Gospel (this explains some of the differences from the conventional version). Other differences are attempts to convey more accurately the meaning of the original. The fact that this version is not known by many in the group unifies the group and encourages people to pay attention to the words of the prayer, so that it is not said mechanically.

Group Guidelines: Review the guidelines for participation by asking each participant to read one. People may discuss the guidelines.

The Eight Tasks: Hand out the list of tasks and share reading by alternating between co-leaders and participants.

What Is the Spirit? Talk about the concept of the spiritual dimension of our lives.

Self-Observation: Go around the circle, asking people to observe three parts of themselves:

- a physical sensation
- an emotion or feeling
- a thought going through their head

(This is practice in self-observation.)

Paired Sharing: Have participants break into pairs, and ask them to discuss briefly "the first time you realized your life had a spiritual dimension."

Sharing about the Sharing: Group discussion by those who would like to share their experience of the paired sharing.

This Week's Task: Read and describe Task 1, noting that the objective of the task is to become aware of your feelings and thoughts. It is a task of self-observation.

Talk: Living in Joy by Becoming Aware.

Closing Thoughts: Comments focused on conclusion, not on opening more discussion.

The Lord's Prayer or Closing: Use music or the new version of the Lord's Prayer to close the session.

Learning Objectives for Task 1

- Understand the concept of the spiritual dimension of life.
- Become familiar with the "house of spiritual awareness" as a model of the mind.
- Understand that uncritical self-awareness and loving self-observation are essential to your spiritual growth.

CENTERING YOURSELF THROUGH MEDITATION

We find that a guided meditation can open our minds to an influx of love and guidance from our Higher Power. Below is a meditation that we use in our groups, with thanks to Louise Rose. This is one of a variety of guided meditations that your group might use.

Guided Meditation

Close your eyes and start to relax. Become aware of your body. Notice any centers of tension that you need to let go of to be comfortable.

Soon you start breathing evenly and gently, in and out. With each inward breath, bring in the life-giving oxygen to fill your lungs, to be carried through your blood to every cell in your body, renewing and revitalizing. This life-giving, loving oxygen feeds your whole body and brings newness and freshness into your life.

And as you breathe out, let go of any negativity, any staleness, anything that you would like to get rid of. Just breathe it out with your breath and it will be gone.

As you continue to breathe gently and evenly, feel your muscles go loose and limp. You find your body getting heavier and heavier and more and more relaxed. Just let go and enjoy that wonderful feeling of relaxation. Notice the oxygen coming into your body and the staleness and negativity going out.

Now notice any thoughts that are floating around in your mind. Give them a moment of attention and then let go. Let them drift off. If they are important, they will come back when you need them. If they're not, let them float away. Soon you have the feeling that your mind is clear and clean, and you begin to feel a mental relaxation to match the physical relaxation in your body.

You begin to approach a deeper part of your being that is always at peace, that is always in touch with your higher self. This part of you is in harmony with the whole universe. It is a peaceful, restful place. This is your retreat where you can come whenever you need it. It is always there for you. This higher level of your being dwells in perfect harmony and looks down on your daily life and passes along its blessings of peace.

All the different parts of God's grand and glorious creation fit together to form a complete and beautiful whole. I am a unique part of God's creation with my own role to fill and my own special gifts to give. The people around me need the gifts I have to give, and more importantly I need to give what is mine to give.

As I open my mind and heart to God I receive new clarity and insight. I see myself as God created me, gifted and talented and needed beyond the furthest stretch of my imagination. I feel welcomed and at one with life wherever I am.

Wherever I go, my personality is the way that I present myself to the world. My body is the vehicle through which my spirit lives and expresses itself. My mind is an instrument for the expression of divine ideas, for I am an eternal spiritual being.

My higher self is undisturbed by outer conditions and circumstances. I remind myself again that I am a spiritual being. I remember that God is my sure and certain guide through all experiences. I know that God is in charge, and I am willing to work with God's plan for good. I am able to express love easily. I know that I am a coworker with God. As a spiritual being I am expressing more and more of God's likeness.

I know that I am a spiritual being, created in the image and likeness of God. On the deepest level, I am at peace and in harmony with the universe. I have a body and I am not my body. I have feelings and I am not my feelings. I have thoughts and I am not my thoughts. I am a beloved child of God, a vessel. The Lord works through me as his instrument. I find my greatest fulfillment when his love passes through me to others who are also his children, who are also created in his image and likeness.

As his love passes through me, I remove those barriers that would stand in its way so that it can flow freely through me to others. I long to remove anything in myself that would impede that flow. I know that I am privileged to be part of the grand plan whereby I can pass on these gifts to others. I feel grateful to be allowed to participate in this great work.

As I place my life in God's hands, I know that I am safe. I know that nothing can harm me, that his loving arms will hold me and embrace me and protect me wherever I go. Thank you, Lord, for loving me.

And now, holding on to that state of peace and harmony, return to this room and to this circle of friends. When you are ready, open your eyes.

1. At meetings, we aim to come from a higher level in ourselves and not from the lower self.

2. We do not give advice.

3. We do not interrupt.

4. We speak only for ourselves.

5. We share; we don't preach.

6. We have the option to pass.

7. There are no failures, only opportunities.

8. We do not use names when sharing about our experiences.

9. We keep confidentiality.

10. We start and end meetings promptly.

THE LORD'S PRAYER

Our Father in heaven, your name must be kept holy. Your kingdom must come. Your will must be done on earth as in heaven.

Give us day by day our daily bread.

And forgive us our sins, for we also forgive everyone who is indebted to us.

And do not lead us into a trial, but deliver us from the evil one.

Amen.

This version of the Lord's Prayer, translated from the original Greek by Jonathan Rose, helps us think about our prayer and see its deeper meaning rather than recite words by rote from memory.

MORE RESOURCES

The Arizona Spiritual Growth Foundation offers recorded lessons and meditations, notes for group leaders, illustrated handouts, and an extensive series of tasks for spiritual growth. Please feel free to contact the ASGF headquarters at Sunrise Chapel if you have any questions about our program.

Arizona Spiritual Growth Foundation, Inc.
8421 East Wrightstown Road, Tucson, AZ 85715

Phone: 520-298-1245

E-mail: asgf@sunrisechapel.org

Our website also offers articles on spiritual growth:
www.angelfire.com/az2/asgf

ABOUT THE PARTICIPANTS

BETSY is a charter member of our "spiritual growth club." She has helped develop many of our tasks as far back as 1988! Her experience as a mother and as an activities director for elderly people gives her rare insight into the struggles of people's spiritual journeys at all ages. Betsy uses spiritual growth principles in all parts of her life, and she credits her continuous work with helping her attain levels of happiness and peace of mind that she could not reach in any other way.

BOB is coauthor of this book (see "About the Authors"). Bob leans heavily on the structure of organized spiritual growth to deal with all the issues in his daily life.

HERB is a retired US Army Operational Command Sergeant with many decorations for his service, including a Purple Heart. A cancer survivor of many years, Herb says that spiritual growth is at the center of his life. He shares our group's tasks with his wife of many years as they attempt to grow together.

JACK is a local radio announcer and newscaster. At the time of this Spiritual Growth Group, he was a few years from retiring, and he knew that daily interaction was one thing he could never retire from. He joined the group to practice, and hear from others, ways to avoid everyday misunderstandings by adopting a more spiritual outlook. He says that, as with previous classes, the techniques mostly worked when he used them and didn't help at all when he forgot or rebelled against them.

JULIE is a caregiver to young nieces. Her daily trials with preteen girls gave her ample opportunity to use the tasks each week, and brought a note of levity to our group discussions. She credits her work on spiritual growth with helping her through her most trying times.

KITTY is an active volunteer and former corporate executive, who moved back to Arizona where in her teens and twenties she had lived on a cattle ranch. Kitty says that staying busy and being useful are keys to her happiness, and she credits spiritual growth work with keeping those values in mind. She joined our group to better understand and enjoy people as they travel their personal spiritual paths. The experience heightened her awareness of people's differences and similarities as we travel on God's path.

LEYLA is a jewelry designer. She says that her roots in Oklahoma and a colorful family have provided her many opportunities to improve her life by using spiritual growth techniques. She loves the group atmosphere and the group sharing.

MICHAEL is a counselor and a member of the US Air Force Reserve, who contributed deep insight and wisdom to our sessions. The work of spiritual growth is central to Mike's daily life; he often calls it "the only game in town!"

TAMI was an administrative assistant at an insurance agency when this group took place, and she is now a teacher for children with special needs. Tami believes that her religion is only as good as her actions; she says she actively works the task on being useful as a central tenet of her life. Her work with charities and church organizations provided our group with wonderful examples of spiritual growth in action.

TRACY is a life counselor and sought-after speaker who uses the principles of spiritual growth in her professional and personal life. In our group meetings, Tracy provided perspective on her own growth and also on how the spiritual growth principles helped her to help others. She credits many sources for her inspiration, but she says the tasks from our Spiritual Growth Group are among the top contributors.

ABOUT THE AUTHORS

FRANK ROSE received his M.Div. from the Academy of the New Church in Bryn Athyn, Pennsylvania, where he also taught. He has served as pastor to groups in England, Scotland, Wales, Holland, Belgium, France, and Canada.

Frank and his wife, Louise, currently live in Tucson, Arizona, where, in 1982, Frank became pastor of the Sunrise Chapel congregation. Noticing a need to apply the teachings of Christianity to everyday life, the Roses and a group of others began the Spiritual Growth Program at the chapel in 1988.

Frank is now Pastor Emeritus of Sunrise Chapel and enjoys his many hobbies in retirement. He has written a number of published works, including *Reflections on Heaven and Hell, Reflections on Providence,* and two field guides, *Mountain Wildflowers of Southern Arizona* and *Mountain Trees of Southern Arizona.* Frank is a founder and the current chairman of the board of the Arizona Spiritual Growth Foundation, Inc.

BOB MAGINEL was born in a small North Dakota town and traveled extensively in his youth. A retired Air Force colonel who served in command and headquarters assignments for over twenty-two years, Bob has resided in many parts of the United States as well as in Europe and Asia. After retirement from the Air Force, he founded Mobility Manufacturing Inc. (a maker of powered wheelchairs) and served as its chairman and CEO until 1994.

Bob holds a BBA in management from the University of Texas and an MS from the Air Force Institute of Technology. He is a graduate of the Armed Forces Staff College and the Air War College.

Bob has led many spiritual growth groups and is a founder of the Arizona Spiritual Growth Foundation, Inc. He currently serves as CEO and board member of the Foundation.

BIBLIOGRAPHY

Works Cited

Lapierre, Dominique. *The City of Joy.* Garden City, NY: Doubleday, 1985.

Nicoll, Maurice. *Psychological Commentaries on the Teachings of Gurdjieff and Ouspensky,* vol. 1. Boston: Shambhala Publications, 1984.

Swedenborg, Emanuel. *Divine Love and Wisdom.* Translated by George F. Dole. West Chester, PA: Swedenborg Foundation, 2003.

———. *Divine Providence.* Translated by George F. Dole. West Chester, PA: Swedenborg Foundation, 2003.

———. *Heaven and Hell.* Translated by George F. Dole. West Chester, PA: Swedenborg Foundation, 2000.

———. *New Jerusalem.* Translated by George F. Dole. West Chester, PA: Swedenborg Foundation, forthcoming.

———. *Revelation Unveiled.* Translated by George F. Dole. 2 vols. West Chester, PA: Swedenborg Foundation, forthcoming.

———. *Secrets of Heaven.* Translated by Lisa Hyatt Cooper. Vols. 1–2. West Chester, PA: Swedenborg Foundation, 2010–12.

———. *Secrets of Heaven.* Translated by Lisa Hyatt Cooper. Vols. 3–15. West Chester, PA: Swedenborg Foundation, forthcoming.

———. *True Christianity.* Translated by Jonathan S. Rose. 2 vols. West Chester, PA: Swedenborg Foundation, 2006–11.

Suggested Reading

Alcoholics Anonymous World Services, Inc. *Alcoholics Anonymous: The Big Book,* 4th ed. New York: A. A. World Services, Inc., 2001.

Chopra, Deepak. *The Ultimate Happiness Prescription: 7 Keys to Joy and Enlightenment.* New York: Harmony Books, 2009.

LeShan, Lawrence. *How to Meditate.* New York: Macmillan Audio, compact disc, 2004.

Rhodes, Peter. *Observing Spirit: Evaluating Your Daily Progress on the Path to Heaven with Gurdjieff and Swedenborg.* West Chester, PA: Swedenborg Foundation, 2005.

Rose, Frank, and Bob Maginel. *The Joy of Spiritual Growth: Real Encounters.* West Chester, PA: Swedenborg Foundation, 1999.

Schnarr, Grant R. *Spiritual Recovery: A Twelve-Step Guide.* West Chester, PA: Swedenborg Foundation, 1998.

Swedenborg, Emanuel. *Regeneration: Spiritual Growth and How It Works.* West Chester, PA: Swedenborg Foundation, 2014.

Taylor, Douglas. *The Hidden Levels of the Mind: Swedenborg's Theory of Consciousness.* West Chester, PA: Swedenborg Foundation, 2011.